MY BOYHOOD
BY
JOHN BURROUGHS

MY BOYHOOD

BY
JOHN BURROUGHS

WITH A CONCLUSION BY
HIS SON
JULIAN BURROUGHS

Fredonia Books
Amsterdam, The Netherlands

My Boyhood

by
John Burroughs

ISBN: 1-58963-472-1

Copyright © 2001 by Fredonia Books

Reprinted from the 1924 edition

Fredonia Books
Amsterdam, The Netherlands
http://www.fredoniabooks.com

All rights reserved, including the right to reproduce this book, or portions thereof, in any form.

In order to make original editions of historical works available to scholars at an economical price, this facsimile of the original edition of 1924 is reproduced from the best available copy and has been digitally enhanced to improve legibility, but the text remains unaltered to retain historical authenticity.

FOREWORD

IN THE beginning, at least, Father wrote these sketches of his boyhood and early farm life as a matter of self-defense: I had made a determined attempt to write them and when I did this I was treading on what was to him more or less sacred ground, for as he once said in a letter to me, "You will be homesick; I know just how I felt when I left home forty-three years ago. And I have been more or less homesick ever since. The love of the old hills and of Father and Mother is deep in the very foundations of my being." He had an intense love of his birthplace and cherished every memory of his boyhood and of his family and of the old farm high up on the side of Old Clump—"the mountain out of whose loins I sprang"—so that when I tried to write of him he felt it was time he took the matter in hand. The following pages are the result.

JULIAN BURROUGHS.

CONTENTS

MY BOYHOOD 1
 By John Burroughs

MY FATHER 135
 By Julian Burroughs

WAITING

Serene, I fold my hands and wait,
Nor care for wind, nor tide, nor sea;
I rave no more 'gainst Time or Fate,
For lo! my own shall come to me.

I stay my haste, I make delays,
For what avails this eager pace?
I stand amid the eternal ways,
And what is mine shall know my face.

Asleep, awake, by night or day,
The friends I seek are seeking me;
No wind can drive my bark astray,
Nor change the tide of destiny.

What matter if I stand alone?
I wait with joy the coming years;
My heart shall reap where it hath sown,
And garner up its fruit of tears.

The waters know their own, and draw
The brook that springs in yonder heights
So flows the good with equal law
Unto the soul of pure delights.

The stars come nightly to the sky;
The tidal wave comes to the sea;
Nor time, nor space, nor deep, nor high,
Can keep my own away from me.

MY BOYHOOD
BY
JOHN BURROUGHS

YOU ask me to give you some account of my life—how it was with me, and now in my seventy-sixth year I find myself in the mood to do so. You know enough about me to know that it will not be an exciting narrative or of any great historical value. It is mainly the life of a country man and a rather obscure man of letters, lived in eventful times indeed, but largely lived apart from the men and events that have given character to the last three quarters of a century. Like tens of thousands of others, I have been a spectator of, rather than a participator in, the activities—political, commercial, sociological, scientific—of the times in which I have lived. My life, like your own, has been along the by-paths rather than along the great public highways. I have known but few great men and have played no part in any great public events—not even in the Civil War which I lived through and in which my duty plainly called me to take part. I am a man who recoils from noise and strife, even from fair competition, and who likes to see his days "linked each to each" by some quiet, congenial occupation.

The first seventeen years of my life were spent on the farm where I was born (1837–1854); the next ten years I was a teacher in rural district schools (1854–1864); then I was for ten years a government clerk in Washington (1864–1873); then in the summer of 1873, while a national bank examiner and bank receiver, I purchased the small fruit farm on the Hudson where you were brought up and where I have since lived, cultivating the land for marketable fruit and the fields and woods for nature literature, as you well know. I have gotten out of my footpaths a few times and traversed some of the great highways of travel—have been twice to Europe, going only as far as Paris (1871 and 1882)—the first time sent to London by the Government with three other men to convey $50,000,000 of bonds to be refunded; the second time going with my family on my own account. I was a member of the Harriman expedition to Alaska in the summer of 1899, going as far as Plover Bay on the extreme N. E. part of Siberia. I was the companion of President Roosevelt on a trip to Yellowstone Park in the spring of 1903. In the winter and spring of 1909 I went to California with two women friends and extended the journey to the Hawaiian Islands, returning home in June. In 1911 I again crossed the continent to California. I have camped and tramped in Maine and in Canada, and have spent part of a winter in Bermuda and in Jamaica. This is an outline of my travels. I have known but few great men. I met Carlyle in the company of Moncure Conway in London in November, 1871. I met Emerson three times—in 1863 at West Point; in 1871 in Baltimore and Washington, where I heard him lecture; and at the Holmes birthday breakfast in Boston in 1879. I knew Walt Whitman intimately from 1863 until his death in 1892. I have met Lowell and Whittier, but not Longfellow or Bryant; I have seen Lincoln, Grant, Sherman, Early, Sumner, Garfield, Cleveland, and other notable men of those days. I heard Tyndall deliver his course of lectures on Light in Washington in 1870 or '71, but missed seeing Huxley during his visit here. I dined with the Rossettis in London in 1871, but was not impressed by them nor they by me. I met Matthew Arnold in New York and heard his lecture on Emerson. My books are, in a way, a record of my life—that part of it that came to flower and fruit in my mind. You could reconstruct my days pretty well from those volumes. A writer who gleans his literary harvest in the fields and woods reaps mainly where he has sown himself. He is a husbandman whose crop springs from the seed of his own heart.

My life has been a fortunate one; I was born under a lucky star. It seems as if both wind and tide had favoured me. I have suffered no great losses, or defeats, or illness, or accidents, and have undergone no great struggles or privations; I have had no grouch, I have not wanted the earth. I am pessimistic by night, but by day I am a confirmed optimist, and it is the days that have stamped my life. I have found this planet a good corner of the universe to live in and I am not in a hurry to exchange it for any other. I hope the joy of living may be as keen with you, my dear boy, as it has been with me and that you may have life on as easy terms as I have. With this foreword I will begin the record in more detail.

I have spoken of my good luck. It began in my being born on a farm, of parents in the prime of their days, and in humble circumstances. I deem it good luck, too, that my birth fell in April, a month in which so many other things find it good to begin life. Father probably tapped the sugar bush about this time or a little earlier; the bluebird and the robin and song sparrow may have arrived that very day. New calves were bleating in the barn and young lambs under the shed. There were earth-stained snow drifts on the hillside, and along the stone walls and through the forests that covered the mountains the coat of snow showed unbroken. The fields were generally bare and the frost was leaving the ground. The stress of winter was over and the warmth of spring began to be felt in the air. I had come into a household of five children, two girls and three boys, the oldest ten years and the youngest two. One had died in infancy, making me the seventh child. Mother was twenty-nine and father thirty-five, a medium-sized, freckled, red-haired man, showing very plainly the Celtic or Welsh strain in his blood, as did mother, who was a Kelly and of Irish extraction on the paternal side. I had come into a family of neither wealth nor poverty as those things were looked upon in those days, but a family dedicated to hard work winter and summer in paying for and improving a large farm, in a country of wide open valleys and long, broad-backed hills and gentle flowing mountain lines; very old geologically, but only one generation from the stump in the history of the settlement. Indeed, the stumps lingered in many of the fields late into my boyhood, and one of my tasks in the dry mid-spring weather was to burn these stumps—an occupation I always enjoyed because the adventure of it made play of the work. The climate was severe in winter, the mercury often dropping to 30° below, though we then had no thermometer to measure it, and the summers, at an altitude of two thousand feet, cool and salubrious. The soil was fairly good, though encumbered with the laminated rock and stones of the Catskill formation, which the old ice sheet had broken and shouldered and transported about. About every five or six acres had loose stones and rock enough to put a rock-bottomed wall around it and still leave enough in and on the soil to worry the ploughman and the mower. All the farms in that section reposing in the valleys and bending up and over the broad-backed hills are checker-boards of stone walls, and the right-angled fields, in their many colours of green and brown and yellow and red, give a striking map-like appearance to the landscape. Good crops of grain, such as rye, oats, buckwheat, and yellow corn, are grown, but grass is the most natural product. It is a grazing country and the dairy cow thrives there, and her products are the chief source of the incomes of the farms.

I had come into a home where all the elements were sweet; the water and the air as good as there is in the world, and where the conditions of life were of a temper to discipline both mind and body. The settlers of my part of the Catskills were largely from Connecticut and Long Island, coming in after or near the close of the Revolution, and with a good mixture of Scotch emigrants.

My great-grandfather, Ephraim Burroughs, came, with his family of eight or ten children, from near Danbury, Conn., and settled in the town of Stamford shortly after the Revolution. He died there in 1818. My grandfather, Eden, came into the town of Roxbury, then a part of Ulster County.

I had come into a land flowing with milk, if not with honey. The maple syrup may very well take the place of the honey. The sugar maple was the dominant tree in the woods and the maple sugar the principal sweetening used in the family. Maple, beech, and birch wood kept us warm in winter, and pine and hemlock timber made from trees that grew in the deeper valleys formed the roofs and the walls of the houses. The breath of kine early mingled with my own breath. From my earliest memory the cow was the chief factor on the farm and her products the main source of the family income; around her revolved the haying and the harvesting. It was for her that we toiled from early July until late August, gathering the hay into the barns or into the stacks, mowing and raking it by hand. That was the day of the scythe and the good mower, of the cradle and the good cradler, of the pitchfork and the good pitcher. With the modern agricultural machinery the same crops are gathered now with less than half the outlay of human energy, but the type of farmer seems to have deteriorated in about the same proportion. The third generation of farmers in my native town are much like the third steeping of tea, or the third crop of corn where no fertilizers have been used. The large, picturesque, and original characters who improved the farms and paid for them are about all gone, and their descendants have deserted the farms or are distinctly of an inferior type. The farms keep more stock and yield better crops, owing to the amount of imported grain consumed upon them, but the families have dwindled or gone out entirely, and the social and the neighbourhood spirit is not the same. No more huskings or quiltings, or apple cuts, or raisings or "bees" of any sort. The telephone and the rural free delivery have come and the automobile and the daily newspaper. The roads are better, communication quicker, and the houses and barns more showy, but the men and the women, and especially the children, are not there. The towns and the cities are now colouring and dominating the country which they have depleted of its men, and the rural districts are becoming a faded replica of town life.

The farm work to which I was early called upon to lend a hand, as I have said, revolved around the dairy cow. Her paths were in the fields and woods, her sonorous voice was upon the hills, her fragrant breath was upon every breeze. She was the centre of our industries. To keep her in good condition, well pastured in summer and well housed and fed in winter, and the whole dairy up to its highest point of efficiency—to this end the farmer directed his efforts. It was an exacting occupation. In summer the day began with the milking and ended with the milking; and in winter it began with the foddering and ended with the foddering, and the major part of the work between and during both seasons had for its object, directly or indirectly, the well-being of the herd. Getting the cows and turning away the cows in summer was usually the work of the younger boys; turning them out of the stable and putting them back in winter was usually the work of the older. The foddering them from the stack in the field in winter also fell to the lot of the older members of the family.

In milking we all took a hand when we had reached the age of about ten years, Mother and my sisters usually doing their share. At first we milked the cows in the road in front of the house, setting the pails of milk on the stone work: later we milked them in a yard in the orchard behind the house, and of late years the milking is done in the stable. Mother said that when they first came upon the farm, as she sat milking a cow in the road one evening, she saw a large black animal come out of the woods out where the clover meadow now is, and cross the road and disappear in the woods on the other side. Bears sometimes carried off the farmers' hogs in those days, boldly invading the pens to do so. My father kept about thirty cows of the Durham breed; now the dairy herds are made up of Jerseys or Holsteins. Then the product that went to market was butter, now it is milk. Then the butter was made on the farm by the farmer's wife or the hired girl, now it is made in the creameries by men. My mother made most of the butter for nearly forty years, packing thousands of tubs and firkins of it in that time. The milk was set in tin pans on a rack in the milk house for the cream to rise, and as soon as the milk clabbered it was skimmed.

About three o'clock in the afternoon during the warm weather Mother would begin skimming the milk, carrying it pan by pan to the big cream pan, where with a quick movement of a case knife the cream was separated from the sides of the pan, the pan tilted on the edge of the cream pan and the heavy mantle of cream, in folds or flakes, slid off into the receptacle and the thick milk emptied into pails to be carried to the swill barrel for the hogs. I used to help Mother at times by handing her the pans of milk from the rack and emptying the pails. Then came the washing of the pans at the trough, at which I also often aided her by standing the pans up to dry and sun on the big bench. Rows of drying tin pans were always a noticeable feature about farmhouses in those days, also the churning machine attached to the milk house and the sound of the wheel, propelled by the "old churner"—either a big dog or a wether sheep. Every summer morning by eight o'clock the old sheep or the old dog was brought and tied to his task upon the big wheel. Sheep were usually more unwilling churners than were the dogs. They rarely acquired any sense of duty or obedience as a dog did. This endless walking and getting nowhere very soon called forth vigorous protests. The churner would pull back, brace himself, choke, and stop the machine: one churner threw himself off and was choked to death before he was discovered. I remember when the old hetchel from the day of flax dressing, fastened to a board, did duty behind the old churner, spurring him up with its score or more of sharp teeth when he settled back to stop the machine. "Run and start the old sheep," was a command we heard less often after that. He could not long hold out against the pressure of that phalanx of sharp points upon his broad rear end.

The churn dog was less obdurate and perverse, but he would sometimes hide away as the hour of churning approached and we would have to hustle around to find him.

But we had one dog that seemed to take pleasure in the task and would go quickly to the wheel when told to and finish his task without being tied. In the absence of both dog and sheep, I have a few times taken their place on the wheel. In winter and early spring there was less cream to churn and we did it by hand, two of us lifting the dasher together. Heavy work for even big boys, and when the stuff was reluctant and the butter would not come sometimes until the end of an hour, the task tried our mettle. Sometimes it would not gather well after it had come, then some deft handling of the dasher was necessary.

I never tired of seeing Mother lift the great masses of golden butter from the churn with her ladle and pile them up in the big butter bowl, with the drops of buttermilk standing upon them as if they were sweating from the ordeal they had been put through. Then the working and the washing of it to free it from the milk and the final packing into tub or firkin, its fresh odour in the air—what a picture it was! How much of the virtue of the farm went each year into those firkins! Literally the cream of the land. Ah, the alchemy of Life, that in the bee can transform one product of those wild rough fields into honey, and in the cow can transform another product into milk!

The spring butter was packed into fifty-pound tubs to be shipped to market as fast as made. The packing into one-hundred-pound firkins to be held over till November did not begin till the cows were turned out to pasture in May. To have made forty tubs by that time and sold them for eighteen or twenty cents a pound was considered very satisfactory. Then to make forty or fifty firkins during the summer and fall and to get as good a price for it made the farmer's heart glad. When Father first came on the farm, in 1827, butter brought only twelve or fourteen cents per pound, but the price steadily crept up till in my time it sold from seventeen to eighteen and a half. The firkin butter was usually sold to a local butter buyer named Dowie. He usually appeared in early fall, always on horseback, having notified Father in advance. At the breakfast table Father would say, "Dowie is coming to try the butter to-day."

"I hope he will not try that firkin I packed that hot week in July," Mother would say. But very likely that was the one among others he would ask for. His long, half-round steel butter probe or tryer was thrust down the centre of the firkin to the bottom, given a turn or two, and withdrawn, its tapering cavity filled with a sample of every inch of butter in the firkin. Dowie would pass it rapidly to and fro under his nose, maybe sometimes tasting it, then push the tryer back into the hole, then withdrawing it, leaving its core of butter where it found it. If the butter suited him, and it rarely failed to do so, he would make his offer and ride away to the next dairy.

The butter had always to be delivered at a date agreed upon, on the Hudson

River at Catskill. This usually took place in November. It was the event of the fall: two loads of butter, of twenty or more firkins each, to be transported fifty miles in a lumber wagon, each round trip taking about four days. The firkins had to be headed up and gotten ready. This job in my time usually fell to Hiram. He would begin the day before Father was to start and have a load headed and placed in the wagon on time, with straw between the firkins so they would not rub. How many times I have heard those loads start off over the frozen ground in the morning before it was light! Sometimes a neighbour's wagon would go slowly jolting by just after or just before Father had started, but on the same errand. Father usually took a bag of oats for his horses and a box of food for himself so as to avoid all needless expenses. The first night would usually find him in Steel's tavern in Greene County, half way to Catskill. The next afternoon would find him at his journey's end and by night unloaded at the steamboat wharf, his groceries and other purchases made, and ready for an early start homeward in the morning. On the fourth night we would be on the lookout for his return. Mother would be sitting, sewing by the light of her tallow dip, with one ear bent toward the road. She usually caught the sound of his wagon first. "There comes your father," she would say, and Hiram or Wilson would quickly get and light the old tin lantern and stand ready on the stonework to receive him and help put out the team. By the time he was in the house his supper would be on the table—a cold pork stew, I remember, used to delight him on such occasions, and a cup of green tea. After supper his pipe, and the story of his trip told, with a list of family purchases, and then to bed. In a few days the second trip would be made. As his boys grew old enough he gave each of them in turn a trip with him to Catskill. It was a great event in the life of each of us. When it came my turn I was probably eleven or twelve years old and the coming event loomed big on my horizon. I was actually to see my first steamboat, the Hudson River, and maybe the steam cars. For several days in advance I hunted the woods for game to stock the provision box so as to keep down the expense. I killed my first partridge and probably a wild pigeon or two and gray squirrels. Perched high on that springboard beside Father, my feet hardly touching the tops of the firkins, at the rate of about two miles an hour over rough roads in chilly November weather, I made my first considerable journey into the world. I crossed the Catskill Mountains and got that surprising panoramic view of the land beyond from the top. At Cairo, where it seems we passed the second night, I disgraced myself in the morning, when Father, after praising me to some bystanders, told me to get up in the wagon and drive the load out in the road. In my earnest effort to do so I ran foul of one side of the big door, and came near smashing things. Father was humiliated and I was dreadfully mortified.

With the wonders of Catskill I was duly impressed, but one of my most vivid remembrances is a passage at arms (verbal) at the steamboat between Father and old Dowie. The latter had questioned the correctness of the weight of the empty firkin which was to be deducted as tare from the total weight. Hot words followed. Father said, "Strip it, strip it." Dowie said, "I will," and in a moment there stood on the scales the naked firkin of butter, sweating drops of salt water. Which won, I do not know. I remember only that peace soon reigned and Dowie continued to buy our butter.

One other incident of that trip still sticks in my mind. I was walking along a street just at dusk, when I saw a drove of cattle coming. The drover, seeing me, called out, "Here, boy, turn those cows up that street!" This was in my line, I was at home with cows, and I turned the drove up in fine style.

As the man came along he said, "Well done," and placed six big copper cents in my hand. Never was my palm more unexpectedly and more agreeably tickled. The feel of it is with me yet!

At an earlier date than that of the accident in the old stone school house, my head, and my body, too, got some severe bruises. One summer day when I could not have been more than three years old, my sister Jane and I were playing in the big attic chamber and amusing ourselves by lying across the vinegar keg and pushing it about the room with our feet. We came to the top of the steep stairway that ended against the chamber door, a foot or more above the kitchen floor, and I suppose we thought it would be fun to take the stairway on the keg. At the brink of that stairway my memory becomes a blank and when I find myself again I am lying on the bed in the "back-bedroom" and the smell of camphor is rank in the room. How it fared with Jane I do not recall; the injury was probably not serious with either of us, but it is easy to imagine how poor Mother must have been startled when she heard that racket on the stairs and the chamber door suddenly burst open, spilling two of her children, mixed up with the vinegar keg, out on the kitchen floor. Jane was more than two years my senior, and should have known better.

Vivid incidents make a lasting impression. I recall what might have been a very serious accident had not my usual good luck attended me, when I was a few years older. One autumn day I was with my older brothers in the corn lot, where they had gone with the lumber wagon to gather pumpkins. When they had got their load and were ready to start I planted myself on the load above the hind axle and let my legs hang down between the spokes of the big wheel. Luckily one of my brothers saw my perilous position just as the team was about to move and rescued me in time. Doubtless my legs would have been broken and maybe very badly crushed in a moment more. But such good fortune seems to have followed me always. One winter's morning, as I stooped to put on one of my boots beside the kitchen stove at the house of a schoolmate with whom I had passed the night, my face came in close contact with the spout of the boiling tea kettle. The scalding steam barely missed my eye and blistered my brow a finger's breadth above it. With one eye gone, I fancy life would have looked quite different. Another time I was walking along one of the market streets of New York, when a heavy bale of hay, through the carelessness of some workman, dropped from thirty or forty feet above me and struck the pavement at my feet. I heard angry words over the mishap, spoken by someone above me, but I only said to myself, "Lucky again!" I recall a bit of luck of a different kind when I was a treasury clerk in Washington. I had started for the seashore for a week's vacation with a small roll of new greenbacks in my pocket. Shortly after the train had left the station

I left my seat and walked through two or three of the forward cars looking for a friend who had agreed to join me. Not finding him, I retraced my steps, and as I was passing along through the car next my own I chanced to see a roll of new bills on the floor near the end of a seat. Instinctively feeling for my own roll of bills and finding it missing, I picked up the money and saw at a glance that it was mine. The passengers near by eyed me in surprise, and I suspect began to feel in their own pockets, but I did not stop to explain and went to my seat startled but happy. I had missed my friend but I might have missed something of more value to me just at that time.

A kind of untoward fate seems inherent in the characters of some persons and makes them the victims of all the ill luck on the road. Such a fate has not been mine. I have met all the good luck on the road. Some kindly influence has sent my best friends my way, or sent me their way. The best thing about me is that I have found a perennial interest in the common universal things which all may have on equal terms, and hence have found plenty to occupy and absorb me wherever I have been. If the earth and the sky are enough for one, why should one sigh for other spheres?

The old farm must have had at least ten miles of stone walls upon it, many of them built new by Father from stones picked up in the fields, and many of them relaid by him, or rather by his boys and hired men. Father was not skilful at any sort of craft work. He was a good ploughman, a good mower and cradler, excellent with a team of oxen drawing rocks, and good at most general farm work, but not an adept at constructing anything. Hiram was the mechanical genius of the family. He was a good wall-layer, and skilful with edged tools. It fell to his lot to make the sleds, the stone-boats, the hay-rigging, the ax helves, the flails, to mend the cradles and rakes, to build the haystacks, and once, I remember, he rebuilt the churning machine. He was slow but he hewed exactly to the line. Before and during my time on the farm Father used to count on building forty or fifty rods of stone wall each year, usually in the spring and early summer. These were the only lines of poetry and prose Father wrote. They are still very legible on the face of the landscape and cannot be easily erased from it. Gathered out of the confusion of nature, built up of fragments of the old Devonian rock and shale, laid with due regard to the wear and tear of time, well-bottomed and well-capped, establishing boundaries and defining possessions, etc., these lines of stone wall afford a good lesson in many things besides wall building. They are good literature and good philosophy. They smack of the soil, they have local colour, they are a bit of chaos brought into order. When you deal with nature only the square deal is worth while. How she searches for the vulnerable points in your structure, the weak places in your foundation, the defective material in your building!

The farmer's stone wall, when well built, stands about as long as he does. It begins to reel and look decrepit when he begins to do so. But it can be relaid and he cannot. One day I passed by the roadside to speak with an old man who was rebuilding a wall. "I laid this wall fifty years ago," he said. "When it is laid up again I shall not have the job." He had stood up longer than had his wall.

A stone wall is the friend of all the wild creatures. It is a safe line of communication with all parts of the landscape. What do the chipmunks, red squirrels, and weasels do in a country without stone fences? The woodchucks and the coons and foxes also use them.

It was my duty as a farm boy to help pick up the stone and pry up the rocks. I could put the bait under the lever, even if my weight on top of it did not count for much. The slow, patient, hulky oxen, how they would kink their tails, hump their backs, and throw their weight into the bows when they felt a heavy rock behind them and Father lifted up his voice and laid on the "gad"! It was a good subject for a picture which, I think, no artist has ever painted. How many rocks we turned out of their beds, where they had slept since the great ice sheet tucked them up there, maybe a hundred thousand years ago—how wounded and torn the meadow or pasture looked, bleeding as it were, in a score of places, when the job was finished! But the further surgery of the plough and harrow, followed by the healing touch of the seasons, soon made all whole again.

The work on the farm in those days varied little from year to year. In winter the care of the cattle, the cutting of the wood, and the thrashing of the oats and rye filled the time. From the age of ten or twelve till we were grown up, we went to school only in winter, doing the chores morning and evening, and engaging in general work every other Saturday, which was a holiday. Often my older brothers would have to leave school by three o'clock to get home to put up the cows in my father's absence. Those school days, how they come back to me!—the long walk across lots, through the snow-choked fields and woods, our narrow path so often obliterated by a fresh fall of snow; the cutting winds, the bitter cold, the snow squeaking beneath our frozen cowhide boots, our trousers' legs often tied down with tow strings to keep the snow from pushing them up above our boot tops; the wide-open white landscape with its faint black lines of stone wall when we had passed the woods and began to dip down into West Settlement valley; the Smith boys and Bouton boys and Dart boys, afar off, threading the fields on their way to school, their forms etched on the white hillsides, one of the bigger boys, Ria Bouton, who had many chores to do, morning after morning running the whole distance so as not to be late; the red school house in the distance by the roadside with the dark spot in its centre made by the open door of the entry way; the creek in the valley, often choked with anchor ice, which our path crossed and into which I one morning slumped, reaching the school house with my clothes freezing upon me and the water gurgling in my boots; the boys and girls there, Jay Gould among them, two thirds of them now dead and the living scattered from the Hudson to the Pacific; the teachers now all dead; the studies, the games, the wrestlings, the baseball—all these things and more pass before me as I recall those long-gone days. Two years ago I hunted up one of those schoolmates in California whom I had not seen for over sixty years. She was my senior by seven or eight years, and I had a boy's remembrance of her fresh sweet face, her kindly eyes and gentle manners. I was greeted by a woman of eighty-two, with dimmed sight and dulled hearing, but instantly I recognized some vestiges of the charm and sweetness of my elder schoolmate of so long ago. No cloud was on her mind or memory and for an hour we again lived among the old people and scenes.

What a roomful of pupils, many of them young men and women, there was during those winters, thirty-five or forty each day! In late years there are never more than five or six. The fountains of population are drying up more rapidly than are our streams. Of that generous roomful of young people, many became farmers, a few became business men, three or four became professional men, and only one, so far as I know, took to letters; and he, judged by his environment and antecedents, the last one you would have picked out for such a career. You might have seen in Jay Gould's Jewish look, bright scholarship, and pride of manners some promise of an unusual career; but in the boy of his own age whom he was so fond of wrestling with and of having go home with him at night, but whose visits he would never return, what was there indicative of the future? Surely not much that I can now discover. Jay Gould, who became a sort of Napoleon of finance, early showed a talent for big business and power to deal with men. He had many characteristic traits which came out even in his walk. One day in New York, after more than twenty years since I had known him as a boy, I was walking up Fifth Avenue, when I saw a man on the other side of the street, more than a block away, coming toward me, whose gait arrested my attention as something I had known long before. Who could it be? I thought, and began to ransack my memory for a clew. I had seen that gait before. As the man came opposite me I saw he was Jay Gould. That walk in some subtle way differed from the walk of any other man I had known. It is a curious psychological fact that the two men outside my own family of whom I have oftenest dreamed in my sleep are Emerson and Jay Gould; one to whom I owe so much, the other to whom I owe nothing; one whose name I revere, the other whose name I associate, as does the world, with the dark way of speculative finance. The new expounders of the philosophy of dreams would probably tell me that I had a secret admiration for Jay Gould. If I have, it slumbers deeply in my sub-conscious self and awakens only when my conscious self sleeps.

But I set out to talk of the work on the farm. The threshing was mostly done in winter with the hickory flail, one shock of fifteen sheaves making a flooring. On the dry cold days the grain shelled easily. After a flooring had been thrashed over at least three times, the straw was bound up again in sheaves, the floor completely raked over and the grain banked up against the side of the bay. When the pile became so large it was in the way, it was cleaned up, that is, run through the fanning mill, one of us shovelling in the grain, another turning the mill, and a third measuring the grain and putting it into bags, or into the bins of the granary. One winter when I was a small boy Jonathan Scudder threshed for us in the barn on the hill. He was in love with my sister Olly Ann and wanted to make a good impression on the "old folks." Every night at supper Father would say to him, "Well, Jonathan, how many shock to-day?" and they grew more and more, until one day he reached the limit of fourteen and he was highly complimented on his day's work. It made an impression on Father, but it did not soften the heart of Olly Ann. The sound of the flail and the fanning mill is heard in the farmers' barns no more. The power threshing machine that travels from farm to farm now does the job in a single day—a few hours of pandemonium, with now and then a hand or an arm crushed in place of the days of leisurely swinging of the hickory flail.

The first considerable work in spring was sugar-making, always a happy time for me. Usually the last half of March, when rills from the melting snow began to come through the fields, the veins of the sugar maples began to thrill with the spring warmth. There was a general awakening about the farm at this time: the cackling of the hens, the bleating of young lambs and calves, and the wistful lowing of the cows. Earlier in the month the "sap spiles" had been overhauled, resharpened, and new ones made, usually from bass wood. In my time the sap gouge was used instead of the auger and the manner of tapping was crude and wasteful. A slanting gash three or four inches long and a half inch or more deep was cut, and an inch below the lower end of this the gouge was driven in to make the place for the spile, a piece of wood two inches wide, shaped to the gouge, and a foot or more in length. It gave the tree a double and unnecessary wound. The bigger the gash the more the sap, seemed to be the theory, as if the tree was a barrel filled with liquid, whereas a small wound made by a half-inch bit does the work just as well and is far less injurious to the tree.

When there came a bright morning, wind northwest and warm enough to begin to thaw by eight o'clock, the sugar-making utensils—pans, kettles, spiles, hogsheads—were loaded upon the sled and taken to the woods, and by ten o'clock the trees began to feel the cruel ax and gouge once more. It usually fell to my part to carry the pans and spiles for one of the tappers, Hiram or Father, and to arrange the pans on a level foundation of sticks or stones, in position. Father often used to haggle the tree a good deal in tapping. "By Fagus," he would say, "how awkward I am!" The rapid tinkle of those first drops of sap in the tin pan, how well I remember it! Probably the note of the first song sparrow or first bluebird, or the spring call of the nuthatch, sounded in unison. Usually only patches of snow lingered here and there in the woods and the earth-stained remnants of old drifts on the sides of the hills and along the stone walls. Those lucid warm March days in the naked maple woods under the blue sky, with the first drops of sap ringing in the pans, had a charm that does not fade from my mind. After the trees were all tapped, two hundred and fifty of them, the big kettles were again set up in the old stone arch, and the hogsheads in which to store the sap placed in position. By four o'clock many of the pans—milk pans from the dairy—would be full, and the gathering with neck yoke and pails began. When I was fourteen or fifteen I took a hand in this part of the work. It used to tax my strength to carry the two twelve-quart pails full through the rough places and up the steep banks in the woods and then lift them up and alternately empty them into the hogsheads without displacing the neck yoke. But I could do it. Now all this work is done by the aid of a team and a pipe fastened on a sled. Before I was old enough to gather sap it fell to me to go to the barns and put in hay for the cows and help stable them. The next morning the boiling of the sap would begin, with Hiram in charge. The big deep iron kettles were slow evaporators compared with the broad shallow sheet-iron pans now in use. Profundity cannot keep up with shallowness in sugar-making, the more superficial your evaporator, within limits, the more rapid your progress. It took the farmers nearly a hundred years to find this out, or at least to act upon it.

At the end of a couple of days of hard boiling Hiram would "syrup off," having reduced two hundred pails of sap to five or six of syrup. The syruping-off often occurred after dark. When the liquid dropped from a dipper which was dipped into it and, held up in the cool air, formed into stiff thin masses, it had reached the stage of syrup. How we minded our steps over the rough path, in the semi-darkness of the old tin lantern, in carrying those precious pails of syrup to the house, where the final process of "sugaring off" was to be completed by Mother and Jane!

The sap runs came at intervals of several days. Two or three days would usually end one run. A change in the weather to below freezing would stop the flow, and a change to much warmer would check it.

The fountains of sap are let loose by frosty sunshine. Frost in the ground, or on it in the shape of snow and the air full of sunshine are the most favourable conditions. A certain chill and crispness, something crystalline, in the air are necessary. A touch of enervating warmth from the south or a frigidity from the north and the trees feel it through their thick bark coats very quickly. Between the temperatures of thirty-five to fifty degrees they get in their best work. After we have had one run ending in rain and warmth, a fresh fall of snow—"sap snow", the farmers call such—will give us another run. Three or four good runs make a long and successful season. My boyhood days in the spring sugar bush were my most enjoyable on the farm. How I came to know each one of those two hundred and fifty trees—what a distinct sense of individuality seemed to adhere to most of them, as much so as to each cow in a dairy! I knew at which trees I would be pretty sure to find a full pan and at which ones a less amount. One huge tree always gave a cream-pan full—a double measure—while the others were filling an ordinary pan. This was known as "the old cream-pan tree." Its place has long been vacant; about half the others are still standing, but with the decrepitude of age appearing in their tops, a new generation of maples has taken the place of the vanished veterans.

While tending the kettles there beside the old arch in the bright, warm March or April days, with my brother, or while he had gone to dinner, looking down the long valley and off over the curving backs of the distant mountain ranges, what dreams I used to have, what vague longings, and, I may say, what happy anticipations! I am sure I gathered more than sap and sugar in those youthful days amid the maples. When I visit the old home now I have to walk up to the sugar bush and stand around the old "boiling place," trying to transport myself back into the magic atmosphere of that boyhood time. The man has his dreams, too, but to his eyes the world is not steeped in romance as it is to the eyes of youth.

One springtime in the sugar season my cousin, Gib Kelly, a boy of my own age, visited me, staying two or three days. (He died last fall.) When he went away I was minding the kettles in the woods, and as I saw him crossing the bare fields in the March sunshine, his steps bent toward the distant mountains, I still remember what a sense of loss came over me, his comradeship had so brightened my enjoyment of the beautiful days. He seemed to take my whole world with him, and on that and the following day I went about my duties in the sap bush in a wistful and pensive mood I had never before felt. I early showed the capacity for comradeship. A boy friend could throw the witchery of romance over everything. Oh, the enchanted days with my youthful mates! And I have not entirely outgrown that early susceptibility. There are persons in the world whose comradeship can still transmute the baser metal of commonplace scenes and experiences into the purest gold of romance for me. It is probably my feminine idiosyncrasies that explain all this. Another unforgettable passion of comradeship in my youth I experienced toward the son of a cousin, a boy four or five years old, or about half my own age. One spring his mother and he were visiting at our house eight or ten days. The child was very winsome and we soon became inseparable companions. He was like a visitor from another sphere. I frequently carried him on my back, and my heart opened to him more and more each day. One day we started to come down a rather steep pair of stairs from the hog-pen chamber; I had stepped down a few steps and reached out to take little Harry in my arms, as he stood on the floor at the head of the stairs, and carry him down, when in his joy he gave a spring and toppled me over with him in my arms, and we brought up at the bottom with our heads against some solid timbers. It was a severe shake-up but hurt my heart more than it did my head because the boy was badly bruised. The event comes back to me as if it were but yesterday. For weeks after his departure I longed for him day and night and the experience still shines like a star in my boyhood life. I never saw him again until two years ago when, knowing he lived there, a practising physician, I hunted him up in San Francisco. I found him a sedate gray-haired man, with no hint, of course, of the child I had known and loved more than sixty years before. It has been my experience on several occasions to hunt up friends of my youth after the lapse of more than half a century. Last spring I had a letter from a pupil of mine in the first school I ever taught, in 1854 or '55. I had not seen or heard from him in all those years when he recalled himself to my mind. The name I had not forgotten, Roswell Beach, but the face I had. Only two weeks ago, being near his town, it occurred to me to look him up. I did so and was shocked to find him on his deathbed. Too weak to raise his head from his pillow he yet threw his arms around me and spoke my name many times with marked affection. He died a few days later. I was to him what some of my old teachers were to me—stars that never set below my horizon.

My boyish liking for girls was quite different from my liking for boys—there was little or no sense of comradeship in it. When I was eight or nine years old there was one girl in the school toward whom I felt very partial, and I thought she reciprocated till one day I suddenly saw how little she cared for me. The teacher had forbidden us to put our feet upon the seats in front of us. In a spirit of rebellion, I suppose, when the teacher was not looking, I put my brown, soil-stained bare feet upon the forbidden seat. Polly quickly spoke up and said, "Teacher, Johnny Burris put his feet on the seat"—what a blow it was to me for her to tell on me! Like a cruel frost those words nipped the tender buds of my affection and they never sprouted again. Years after, her younger brother married my younger sister, and maybe that unkind cut of our school days kept me from marrying Polly. I had other puppy loves but they all died a natural death.

But let me get back to the farm work.

The gathering of the things in the sugar bush, when the flow of sap had stopped, usually fell to Eden and me. We would carry the pans and spiles together in big piles, where the oxen and sled could reach them. Then when they were taken to the house it was my mother's and sister's task to get them ready for the milk.

The drawing out of the manure and the spring ploughing was the next thing in order on the farm. I took a hand in the former but not in the latter. The spreading of the manure that had been drawn out and placed in heaps in the fields during the winter often fell to me. I remember that I did not bend my back to the work very willingly, especially when the cattle had been bedded with long rye straw, but there were compensations. I could lean on my fork handle and gaze at the spring landscape, I could see the budding trees and listen to the songs of the early birds and maybe catch the note of the first swallow in the air overhead. The farm boy always has the whole of nature at his elbow and he is usually aware of it.

When, armed with my long-handled "knocker," I used to be sent forth in the April meadows to beat up and scatter the fall droppings of the cows—the Juno's cushions as Irving named them—I was in much more congenial employment. Had I known the game of golf in those days I should probably have looked upon this as a fair substitute. To stand the big cushions up on edge and with a real golfer's swing hit them with my mallet and see the pieces fly was more like play than work. Oh, then it was April and I felt the rising tide of spring in my blood, and a bit of free activity like this under the blue sky suited my humour. A boy likes almost any work that affords him an escape from routine and humdrum and has an element of play in it. Turning the grindstone or the fanning mill or carrying together sheaves or picking up potatoes or carrying in wood were duties that were a drag upon my spirits.

The spring ploughing and the sowing of the grain and harrowing fell mainly to Father and my older brothers. The spring work was considered done when the oats were sowed and the corn and potatoes planted: the first in early May, the latter in late May. The buckwheat was not sown until late June. One farmer would ask another, "How many oats are you going to sow, or have you sown?" not how many acres. "Oh, fifteen or twenty bushels," would be the answer.

The working of the roads came in June after the crops were in. All hands, summoned by the "path master," would meet at a given date, at the end of the district down by the old stone school house—men and boys with oxen, horses, scrapers, hoes, crowbars—and begin repairing the highway. It was not strenuous work, but a kind of holiday that we all enjoyed more or less. The road got fixed after a fashion, here and there—a bridge mended, a ditch cleaned out, the loose stones removed, a hole filled up, or a short section "turnpiked"—but the days were eight-hour days and they did not sit heavy upon us. The state does it much better now with road machinery and a few men. Once or twice a year Father used to send me with a hoe to throw the loose stones out of the road.

A pleasanter duty during those years was shooting chipmunks around the corn. These little rodents were so plentiful in my youth that they used to pull up the sprouting corn around the margin of the field near the stone walls. Armed with the old flint-lock musket, sometimes loaded with a handful of hard peas, I used to haunt the edges of the cornfield, watching for the little striped-backed culprits. How remorselessly I used to kill them! In those days there were a dozen where there is barely one now. The woods literally swarmed with them, and when beechnuts and acorns were scarce they were compelled to poach upon the farmer's crops. It was to reduce them and other pests that shooting matches were held. Two men would choose sides as in the spelling matches, seven or eight or more were on a side, and the side that brought in the most trophies at the end of the week won and the losing side had to pay for the supper at the village hotel for the whole crowd. A chipmunk's tail counted one, a red squirrel's three, a gray squirrel's still more. Hawks' heads and owls' heads counted as high as ten, I think. Crows' heads also counted pretty high. One man who had little time to hunt engaged me to help him, offering me so much per dozen units. I remember that I found up in the sap bush a brood of young screech owls just out of the nest and I killed them all. That man is still owing me for those owls. What a lot of motley heads and tails were brought in at the end of the week! I never saw them but wish I had. Repeated shooting matches of this kind, in different parts of the state, so reduced the small wild life, especially the chipmunks, that it has not yet recovered, and probably never will. In those days the farmer's hand was against nearly every wild thing. We used to shoot and trap crows and hen hawks and small hawks as though they were our mortal enemies. Farmers were wont to stand up poles in their meadows and set steel traps on the top of them to catch the hen hawks that came for the meadow mice which were damaging their meadows. The hen hawk is so named because he rarely or never catches a hen or a chicken. He is a mouser. We used to bait the hungry crows in spring with "deacon" legs and shoot them without mercy, and all because they now and then pulled a little corn, forgetting or not knowing of the grubs and worms they pulled and the grasshoppers they ate. But all this is changed and now our sable friends and the high-soaring hawks are seldom molested. The fool with a rifle is very apt to shoot an eagle if the chance comes to him, but he has to be very sly about it.

The buttercups and the daisies would be blooming when we were working the road, and the timothy grass about ready to do so —pointing to the near approach of the great event of the season, the one major task toward which so many other things pointed —"haying;" the gathering of our hundred or more tons of meadow hay. This was always a hard-fought campaign. Our weapons were gotten ready in due time, new scythes and new snaths, new rakes and new forks, the hay riggings repaired or built anew, etc. Shortly after the Fourth of July the first assault upon the legions of timothy would be made in the lodged grass below the barn. Our scythes would turn up great swaths that nearly covered the ground and that put our strength to a severe test. When noon came we would go to the house with shaking knees.

The first day of haying meant nearly a whole day with the scythe, and was the most trying of all. After that a half day mowing, when the weather was good, meant work in curing and hauling each afternoon. From the first day in early July till the end of August we lived for the hayfield. No respite except on rainy days and Sundays, and no change except from one meadow to another. No eight-hour days then, rather twelve and fourteen, including the milking. No horse rakes, no mowing machines or hay tedders or loading or pitching devices then. The scythe, the hand rake, the pitchfork in the calloused hands of men and boys did the work, occasionally the women even taking a turn with the rake or in mowing away. I remember the first wire-toothed horse rake with its two handles, which when the day was hot and the grass heavy nearly killed both man and horse. The holder would throw his weight upon it to make it

MY BOYHOOD 55

grip and hold the hay, and then, in a spasm of energy, lift it up and make it drop the hay. From this rude instrument, through various types of wooden and revolving rakes, the modern wheeled rake, with which the raker rides at his ease, has been evolved. At this season the cows were brought to the yard by or before five, breakfast was at six, lunch in the field at ten, dinner at twelve, and supper at five, with milking and hay drawing and heaping up till sundown. Those mid-forenoon lunches of Mother's good rye bread and butter, with crullers or gingerbread, and in August a fresh green cucumber and a sweating jug of water fresh from the spring—sweating, not as we did, because it was hot, but because it was cold, partaken under an ash or a maple tree—how sweet and fragrant the memory of it all is to me!

Till I reached my 'teens it was my task to spread hay and to rake after; later I took my turn with the mowers and pitchers. I never loaded, hence I never pitched over the big beam. How Father watched the weather! The rain that makes the grass ruins the hay. If the morning did not promise a good hay day our scythes would be ground but hung back in their places. When a thunderstorm was gathering in the west and much hay was ready for hauling, how it quickened our steps and our strokes! It was the sound of the guns of the approaching foe. In one hour we would do, or try to do, the work of two. How the wagon would rattle over the road, how the men would mop their faces and how I, while hurrying, would secretly exult that now I would have an hour to finish my crossbow or to work on my pond in the pasture lot!

Those late summer afternoons after the shower—what man who has spent his youth on the farm does not recall them! The high-piled thunder heads of the retreating storm above the eastern mountains, the moist fresh smell of the hay and the fields, the red puddles in the road, the robins singing from the tree tops, the washed and cooler air and the welcomed feeling of relaxation which they brought. It was a good time now to weed the garden, to grind the scythes, and do other odd jobs.

When the haying was finished, usually late in August, in my time, there was usually a let-up for a few days.

I was the seventh child in a family of ten children: Hiram, Olly Ann, Wilson, Curtis, Edmond, and Jane came before me; Eden, Abigail, and Eveline came after me. All were as unlike me in those mental qualities by which I am known to the world as you can well conceive, but all were like me in their more fundamental family traits. We all had the same infirmities of character: we were all tenderfeet—lacking in grit, will power, self-assertion, and the ability to deal with men. We were easily crowded to the wall, easily cheated, always ready to take a back seat, timid, complying, undecided, obstinate but not combative, selfish but not self-asserting, always the easy victims of pushing, coarse-grained, designing men. As with Father, the word came easy but the blow was slow to follow. Only a year or two ago a lightning-rod man made my brother Curtis and his son John have his rods put upon their barn against their wills. They did not want his rods but could not say "No" with enough force. He simply held them up and made them take his rods, willy nilly. Curtis had maps, books, washing machines, etc., forced upon him in the same way. I am able to resist the tree men, book agents, etc., and the lightning-rod man, for a wonder, found me a decided non-conductor; but I can see how my weaker brothers failed. I have settled a lawsuit rather than fight it out when I knew law and justice were on my side. My wife has often said that I never knew when I was imposed upon. I may know it and yet feel that resenting it would cause me more pain than the affront did. Strife and contention kill me, yet come easy to me, and did to all my family. My sense of personal dignity, personal honour, is not a plant of such tender growth that it cannot stand rough winds and nipping frosts. That is a flattering way of saying that we are a very non-chivalrous tribe and would rather run away than fight any time. During the anti-rent war in Delaware County in 1844, Father, who was a "down renter," once fled to a neighbour's house when he saw the posse coming and took refuge under the bed, leaving his feet sticking out. Father never denied it and never seemed a bit humiliated when twitted about it. Grandfather Kelly seems to have used up all our fighting blood in campaigning with Washington, though I more than half suspect that our noncombativeness comes from the paternal side of the family. As a school boy I never had a fight, nor have I ever dealt or received a hostile blow since. And I never saw but one of my brothers fight at school, and he fought the meanest boy in school and punished him well. I can see him now, sitting on the prostrate form of the boy, with his hands clinched in the boy's hair and jamming his face down into the crusty snow till the blood streamed down his face. The nearest I ever came to a fight at school was when, one noontime, we were playing baseball and a boy of my own age and size got angry at me and dared me to lay my hand on him. I did it quickly, but his bite did not follow his bark. I was never whipped at school or at home that I can remember, though I no doubt often deserved it. There was a good deal of loud scolding in our family but very few blows.

Father and Mother had a pretty hard struggle to pay for the farm and to clothe and feed and school us all. We lived off the products of the farm to an extent that people do not think of doing nowadays. Not only was our food largely home grown but our clothes also were home grown and home spun. In my early youth our house linen and our summer shirts and trousers were made from flax that grew on the farm. Those pioneer shirts, how vividly I remember them! They dated from the stump, and bits of the stump in the shape of "shives" were inwoven in their texture and made the wearer of them an unwilling penitent for weeks, or until use and the washboard had subdued them. Peas in your shoes are no worse than "shives" on your shirt. But those tow shirts stood by you. If you lost your hold in climbing a tree and caught on a limb your shirt or your linen trousers would hold you. The stuff from which they were made had a history behind it—pulled up by the roots, rooted on the ground, broken with a crackle, flogged with a swingle, and drawn through a hetchel, and out of all this ordeal came the flax. How clearly I remember Father working with it in the bright, sharp March days, breaking it, then swingling it with a long wooden sword-like tool over the end of an upright board fixed at the base in a heavy block. This was to separate the brittle fragments of the bark from the fibres of the flax. Then in large handfuls he drew it through the hetchel—an instrument with a score or more long sharp iron teeth, set in a board, row behind row. This combed out the tow and other worthless material. It was a mighty good discipline for the flax; it straightened out its fibres and made it as clear and straight as a girl's tresses. Out of the tow we twisted bag strings, flail strings, and other strings. With the worthless portions we made huge bonfires. The flax, Mother would mass upon her distaff and spin into threads. The last I saw of the old crackle, fifty or more years ago, it served as a hen roost under the shed, and the savage old hetchel was doing duty behind the old churner when he sulked and pulled back so as to stop the churning machine. It was hetcheling wool then instead of flax. The flax was spun on a quill which ran by the foot and the quills or spools holding the thread were used in a shuttle when the cloth was woven. The old loom stood in the hog-pen chamber, and there Mother wove her linen, her rag carpets, and her woollen goods. I have "quilled" for her many a time—that is, run the yarn off the reel into spools for use in the shuttle.

Father had a flock of sheep which yielded wool enough for our stockings, mittens, comforts, and underwear, and woollen sheets and comforts for the beds. I have some of those home-made woollen sheets and bed covers now at Slabsides.

Before the sheep were sheared in June they were driven two miles to the creek to be washed. Washing-sheep-day was an event on the farm. It was no small task to get the sheep off the mountain, drive them to the deep pool behind old Jonas More's grist mill, pen them up there, and drag them one by one into the water and make good clean Baptists of them! But sheep are no fighters, they struggle for a moment and then passively submit to the baptism. My older brothers usually did the washing and I the herding. When the shearing was done, a few days later the poor creatures were put through another ordeal, to which after a brief struggle they quickly resigned themselves. Father did the shearing, while I at times held the animal's legs. Father was not an adept hand with the shears and the poor beast usually had to part with many a bit of her hide along with her fleece. It used to make me wince as much as it did the sheep to see the crests of those little wrinkles in her skin clipped off.

I used to wonder how the sheep knew one another and how the lambs knew their mothers when shorn of their fleeces. But they did. The wool was soon sent to the fulling mill and made into rolls, though I have seen it carded and made into rolls at home by hand. How many bundles of rolls tied up into sheets I have seen come home! Then in the long summer afternoons I would hear the hum of the big spinning wheel in the chamber and hear the tread of the girl as she ran it, walking to and fro and drawing out and winding up the yarn. The white rolls, ten inches or more long and the thickness of one's finger, would lie in a pile on the beam of the wheel and one by one would be attached to the spindle and drawn out into yarn of the right size. Each new roll was welded on to the end of the one that went before it so that the yarn did not show the juncture. But now for more than sixty years the music of the spinning wheel has not been heard in the land.

Mother used to pick her geese in the barn where Father used to shear the sheep; and to help gather in the flock was a part of my duty also. The geese would submit to the plucking about as readily as the sheep to the shearing, but they presented a much more ragged and sorry appearance after they had been fleeced than did the sheep. It used to amuse me to see them put their heads together and talk it over and laugh and congratulate each other over the victory they had just won!—they had got out of the hands of the enemy with only the loss of a few feathers which they would not want in the warm weather! The goose is the one inhabitant that cackles as loudly and as cheerfully over a defeat as over a victory. They are so complacent and optimistic that it is a comfort to me to see them about. The very silliness of the goose is a lesson in wisdom. The pride of a plucked gander makes one take courage. I think it quite probable that we learned our habit of hissing our dissent from the goose, and maybe our other habit of trying sometimes to drown an opponent with noise has a like origin. The goose is silly and shallow-pated; yet what dignity and impressiveness in her migrating wild clans driving in ordered ranks across the spring or autumnal skies, linking the Chesapeake Bay and the Canadian Lakes in one flight! The great forces are loosened and winter is behind them in one case, and the tides of spring bear them on in the other. When I hear the trumpet of the wild geese in the sky I know that dramatic events in the seasonal changes are taking place.

I was the only one of the ten children who, as Father said, "took to larnin'," though in seventy-five years of poring over books and periodicals I have not become "learned." But I easily distanced the other children in school. The others barely learned to read and write and cipher a little, Curtis and Wilson barely that, Hiram got into Greenleaf's Grammar and learned to parse, but never to write or speak correctly, and he ciphered nearly through Dayball's Arithmetic. I went through Dayball and then Thompkins and Perkins and got well on into algebra in the district school. My teacher, however, when I was about thirteen or fourteen, did not seem much impressed by my aptitude, for I recall that he told other scholars, boys and girls of about my own age, to get them each a grammar, but did not tell me. I felt a little slighted but made up my mind I would have a grammar also. Father refusing to buy it for me, I made small cakes of maple sugar in the spring and, peddling them in the village, got money enough to buy the grammar and other books. The teacher was a little taken aback when I produced my book as the others did theirs, but he put me in the class and I kept along with the rest of them, but without any idea that the study had any practical bearing on our daily speaking and writing. That teacher was a superior man, a graduate of the state normal school at Albany, but I failed to impress him with my scholarly aptitudes, which certainly were not remarkable. But long afterward, when he had read some of my earlier magazine articles, he wrote to me, asking if I were indeed his early farm boy pupil. His interest and commendation gave me rare pleasure. I had at last justified that awkward intrusion into his grammar class. Much later in life, after he had migrated to Kansas, while on a visit East he called upon me when I chanced to be in my native town. This gave me a still deeper pleasure. He died in Kansas many years ago and is buried there. I have journeyed through the state many times and always remember that it holds the ashes of my old teacher. It is a satisfaction for me to write his name, James Oliver, in this record.

I was in many respects an odd one in my father's family. I was like a graft from some other tree. And this is always a disadvantage to a man—not to be the logical outcome of what went before him, not to be backed up by his family and inheritance —to be of the nature of a sport. It seems as if I had more intellectual capital than I was entitled to and robbed some of the rest of the family, while I had a full measure of the family weaknesses. I can remember how abashed I used to be as a child when strangers or relatives, visiting us for the first time, after looking the rest of the children over, would ask, pointing to me, "That is not your boy—whose is he?" I have no idea that I looked different from the others, because I can see the family stamp upon my face very plainly until this day. My face resembles Hiram's more than any of the others, and I have a deeper attachment for him than for any of the rest of my brothers. Hiram was a dreamer, too, and he had his own idealism which expressed itself in love of bees, of which he kept many hives at one time, and of fancy stock, sheep, pigs, poultry, and a desire to see other lands. His bees and fancy stock never paid him, but he always expected they would the next year. But they yielded him honey and wool of a certain intangible, satisfying kind. To be the owner of a Cotswold ram or ewe for which he had paid one hundred dollars or more gave him rare satisfaction. One season, in his innocence, he took some of his fancy sheep to the state fair at Syracuse, not knowing that an unknown outsider stood no chance at all on such an occasion.

Hiram always had to have some sort of a plaything. Though no hunter and an indifferent marksman, he had during his life several fancy rifles. Once when he came to Washington to visit me, he brought his rifle with him, carrying the naked weapon in his hand or upon his shoulder. The act was merely the whim of a boy who likes to take his playthings with him. Hiram certainly had not come to "shoot up" the town. In the early '60's he had a fifty-dollar rifle made by a famous rifle maker in Utica. There was some hitch or misunderstanding about it and Hiram made the trip to Utica on foot. I was at home that summer and I recall seeing him start off one June day, wearing a black coat, bent on his fifty-mile walk to see about his pet rifle. Of course nothing came of it. The rifle maker had Hiram's money, and he put him off with fair words; then something happened and the gun never came to Hiram's hand.

Another plaything of his was a kettle drum with which he amused himself in the summer twilight for many seasons. Then he got a bass drum which Curtis learned to play, and a very warlike sound often went up from the peaceful old homestead. When I was married and came driving home one October twilight with my wife, the martial music began as soon as we hove in sight of the house. Early in the Civil War, Hiram seriously talked of enlisting as a drummer, but Father and Mother dissuaded him. I can see what a wretched homesick boy he would have been before one week had passed. For many years he was haunted with a desire to go West, and made himself really believe that the next month or the month after he would go. He kept his valise packed under his bed for more than a year, to be ready when the impulse grew strong enough. One fall it became strong enough to start him and carried him as far as White Pigeon, Michigan, where it left him stranded. After visiting a cousin who lived there he came back, and henceforth his Western fever assumed only a low, chronic type.

I tell you all these things about Hiram

because I am a chip out of the same block and see myself in him. His vain regrets, his ineffectual resolutions, his day-dreams, and his playthings—do I not know them all?—only nature in some way dealt a little more liberally with me and made many of my dreams come true. The dear brother!—he stood next to Father and Mother to me. How many times he broke the path for me through the winter snows on the long way to school! How faithful he was to write to me and to visit me wherever I was, after I left home! How he longed to follow my example and break away from the old place but could never quite screw his courage up to the sticking point! He never read one of my books but he rejoiced in all the good fortune that was mine. Once when I was away at school and fell short of money, Hiram sent me a small sum when Father could not or would not send. In later life he got it paid back manyfold—and what a satisfaction it was to me thus to repay him!

Hiram was always a child, he never grew up, which is true of all of us, more or less, and true of Father also. I was an odd one, but I shared all the family infirmities. In fact, I have always been an odd one amid most of my human relations in life. Place me in a miscellaneous gathering of men and I separate from them, or they from me, like oil from water. I do not mix readily with my fellows. I am not conscious of drawing into my shell, as the saying is, but I am conscious of a certain strain put upon me by those about me. I suppose my shell or my skin is too thin. Burbank experimented with walnuts trying to produce one with a thin shell, till he finally produced one with so thin a shell that the birds ate it up. Well, the birds eat me up for the same reason, if I don't look out. I am social but not gregarious. I do not thrive in clubs, I do not smoke, or tell stories, or drink, or dispute, or keep late hours. I am usually as solitary as a bird of prey, though I trust not for the same reason. I love

MY BOYHOOD 75

so much to float on the current of my own thoughts. I mix better with farmers, workers, and country people generally than with professional or business men. Birds of a feather do flock together, and if we do not feel at ease in our company we may be sure we are in the wrong flock. Once while crossing the continent at some station in Minnesota a gray-bearded farmer-like man got on the train and presently began to look eagerly about the Pullman as if to see what kind of company he was in. After a while his eye settled on me at the other end of the car. In a few minutes he came over to me and sat down beside me and began to tell me his story. He had come from Germany as a young man and had lived fifty years on a farm in Minnesota and now he was going back to visit the country of his birth. He had prospered and had left his sons in charge of his farm. What an air he had of a boy out of school! The adventure was warming his blood; he was going home and he wanted someone to whom he could tell the good news. I was probably the only real countryman in the car and he picked me out at once, some quality of rural things hovered about us both and drew us together. I felt that he had paid me an involuntary compliment. How unsophisticated and communicative he was! So much so that I took it upon myself to caution him against the men he was liable to fall in with in New York. I should like to know if he reached the fatherland safely and returned to his Minnesota farm.

When I was a boy six or seven years old a quack phrenologist stopped at our house and Father kept him over night. In the morning he fingered the bumps of all of us to pay for his lodging and breakfast. When he came to my head I remember he grew enthusiastic. "This boy will be a rich man," he said. "His head beats 'em all." And he enlarged on the great wealth I was to accumulate. I forget the rest; but that my bumps were nuggets of gold under the quack's fingers, this

I have not forgotten. The prophecy never came true, though more money did come my way than to any of the rest of the family. Three of my brothers, at least, were not successful from a business point of view, and while I myself have failed in every business venture I ever undertook—beginning with that first speculative stroke sometime in the 'forties when, one March morning, I purchased the prospective sap of Curtis's two maple trees for four cents; yet a certain success from a bread-and-butter point of view has been mine. Father took less stock in me than in the other boys —mainly, I suppose, on account of my early proclivity for books; hence it was a deep satisfaction to me, when his other sons had failed him and loaded the old farm with debt, that I could come back and be able to take the burden of the debts upon myself and save the farm from going into strange hands. But it was my good fortune, a kind of constitutional good luck and not any business talent that enabled me to do so. Remembering the prediction of the old quack phrenologist, I used to have my dreams when a boy, especially on one occasion, I remember, when I was tending the sap kettles in the sugar bush on a bright April day, of gaining great wealth and coming home in imposing style and astonishing the natives with my display. How different the reality from the boy's dream! I came back indeed with a couple of thousand dollars in my pocket (on my bank book), sorrowing and oppressed, more like a pilgrim doing penance than like a conqueror returning from his victories. But we kept the old farm, and as you know, it still plays an important part in my life though I passed the title to my brother many years ago. It is my only home, other homes that I have had were mere camping places for a day and night. But the wealth which my bumps indicated turned out to be of a very shadowy and uncommercial kind, yet of a kind that thieves cannot steal or panics disturb.

I remember the first day I went to school, probably near my fifth year. It was at the old stone school house, about one and a half miles from home. I recall vividly the suit Mother made for the occasion out of some striped cotton goods with a pair of little flaps or hound's ears upon my shoulders that tossed about as I ran. I accompanied Olly Ann, my oldest sister. At each one of the four houses we passed on the way I asked, "Who lives there?" I have no recollection of what happened at school those first days, but I remember struggling with the alphabet soon thereafter; the letters were arranged in a column, the vowels first, a, e, i, o, u, and then the consonants. The teacher would call us to her chair three or four times a day, and opening the Cobb's spelling-book, point to the letters one by one and ask me to name them, drilling them into me in that way. I remember that one of the boys, older than I, Hen Meeker, on one occasion stuck on "e." "I'll bet little Johnny Burris can tell what that letter is. Come up here, Johnny." Up I went and promptly answered, to the humiliation of Hen, "e." "I told you so," said the school marm. How long it took me to learn the alphabet in this arbitrary manner I do not know. But I remember tackling the a, b, abs, and slowly mastering those short columns. I remember also getting down under the desk and tickling the bare ankles of the big girls that sat in the seat in front of me.

The summer days were long and little boys must sit on the hard seats and be quiet and go out only at the regular recess. The seat I sat on was a slab turned flat side up and supported on four legs cut from a sapling. My feet did not touch the floor and I suppose I got very tired. One afternoon the oblivion of sleep came over me and when I came to consciousness again I was in a neighbour's house on a couch and the "smell of camphor pervaded the room." I had fallen off the seat backward and hit my head on the protruding stones of the unplastered wall behind me and cut a hole in it, and I suppose for the moment effectively scattered my childish wits. But Mrs. Reed was a motherly body and consoled me with flowers and sweets and bathed my wounds with camphor and I suppose little Johnny was soon himself again. I have often wondered if a small bony protuberance on the back of my head dated from that collision with the old stone school house.

Another early remembrance connected with the old stone school house is that of seeing Hiram, during the summer noons, catch fish in a pail back of old Jonas More's grist mill and put them in the pot holes in the red sandstone rocks, to be kept there till we went home at night. Then he took them in his dinner pail and put them in his pond down in the pasture lot. I suspect that it was this way that chubs were introduced into the West Settlement trout stream. The fish used to swim around and around in the pot holes seeking a way to escape. I would put my finger into the water but jerk it back quickly as the fish came around. I was afraid of them. But before that I was once scared into a panic by a high-soaring hen hawk. I have probably pointed out to you where, one summer day, as I was going along the road out on what we called the big hill, I looked skyward and saw a big hen hawk describing his large circles about me. A sudden fear fell upon me, and I took refuge behind the stone wall. Still earlier in my career I had my first panic farther along on this same road. I suppose I had started off on my first journey to explore the world when, getting well down the Deacon road beside the woods, I looked back and, seeing how far I was from home, was seized with a sudden consternation and turned and ran back as fast as I could go. I have seen a young robin do the same thing when it had wandered out a yard or so on the branch away from its nest.

I mastered only my a-b-c's at the old

stone school house. A year or two later we were sent off in the West Settlement district and I went to school at a little unpainted school house with a creek on one side of it and toeing squarely on the highway on the other. This also was about one and a half miles from home, an easy, adventurous journey in the summer with the many allurements of fields, stream, and wood, but in winter often a battle with snow and cold. In winter we went across lots, my elder brothers breaking a path through the fields and woods. How the tracks in the snow—squirrels, hares, skunks, foxes—used to excite my curiosity! And the line of ledges off on the left in the woods where brother Wilson used to set traps for skunks and coons—how they haunted my imagination as I caught dim glimpses of them, trudging along in our narrow path! One mild winter morning, after I had grown to be a boy of twelve or thirteen, my younger brother and I had an adventure with a hare. He sat in his form in the deep snow between the roots of a maple tree that stood beside the path. We were almost upon him before we discovered him. As he did not move I withdrew a few yards to a stone wall and armed myself with a boulder the size of my fist. Returning, I let drive, sure of my game, but I missed by a foot, and the hare bounded away over the wall and out into the open and off for the hemlocks a quarter of a mile away. A rabbit in his form only ten feet away does not so easily become a rabbit in the hand. This desire of the farm boy to slay every wild creature he saw was universal in my time. I trust things have changed in this respect since then.

At the little old school house I had many teachers, Bill Bouton, Bill Allaben, Taylor Grant, Jason Powell, Rossetti Cole, Rebecca Scudder, and others. I got well into Dayball's Arithmetic, Olney's Geography, and read Hall's History of the United States— through the latter getting quite familiar with the Indian wars and the French war and the Revolution. Some books in the district library also attracted me. I think I was the only one of the family that took books from the library. I recall especially "Murphy, the Indian Killer" and the "Life of Washington." The latter took hold of me; I remember one summer Sunday, as I was playing through the house with my older brothers, of stopping to read a certain passage of it aloud, and that it moved me so that I did not know whether I was in the body or out. Many times I read that passage and every time I was submerged, as it were, by a wave of emotion. I mention so trifling a matter only to show how responsive I was to literature at an early age. I should perhaps offset this statement by certain other facts which are by no means so flattering. There was a period in my latter boyhood when comic song-books, mostly of the Negro minstrely sort, satisfied my craving for poetic literature. I used to learn the songs by heart and invent and extemporize tunes for them.

To this day I can repeat some of those rank Negro songs.

My taste for books began early, but my taste for good literature was of a much later and of slow growth. My interest in theological and scientific questions antedated my love of literature. During the last half of my 'teens I was greatly interested in phrenology and possessed a copy of Spurzheim's "Phrenology," and of Comb's "Constitution of Man." I also subscribed to Fowler's *Phrenological Journal* and for years accepted the phrenologists' own estimate of the value of their science. And I still see some general truths in it. The size and shape of the brain certainly give clues to the mind within, but its subdivision into many bumps, or numerous small areas, like a garden plot, from each one of which a different crop is produced, is absurd. Certain bodily functions are localized in the brain, but not our mental and emotional traits—veneration, self-esteem, sublimity— these are attributes of the mind as a unit.

As I write these lines I am trying to see wherein I differed from my brothers and from other boys of my acquaintance. I certainly had a livelier interest in things and events about me. When Mr. McLaurie proposed to start an academy in the village and came there to feel the pulse of the people and to speak upon the subject I believe I was the only boy in his audience. I was probably ten or twelve years of age. At one point in his address the speaker had occasion to use me to illustrate his point: "About the size of that boy there," he said, pointing to me, and my face flushed with embarrassment. The academy was started and I hoped in a few years to attend it. But the time when Father could see his way to send me there never came. One season when I was fifteen or sixteen, I set my heart on going to school at Harpersfield. A boy whom I knew in the village attended it and I wanted to accompany him. Father talked encouragingly and held it out as a possible reward if I helped hurry the farm work along. This I did, and for the first time taking to field with the team and plough and "summer fallowing" one of the oat-stubble lots. I followed the plough those September days with dreams of Harpersfield Academy hovering about me, but the reality never came. Father concluded, after I had finished my job of ploughing, that he could not afford it. Butter was low and he had too many other ways for using his money. I think it quite possible that my dreams gave me the best there was in Harpersfield anyway—a worthy aspiration is never lost. All these things differentiate me from my brothers.

My interest in theological questions showed itself about the same time. An itinerant lecturer with a smooth, ready tongue came to the village charged with novel ideas about the immortality of the soul, accepting the literal truth of the text "The soul that sinneth, it shall die." I attended the meetings and took notes of the speaker's glib talk. I distinctly remember that it was from his mouth that I first heard the word "encyclopædia." When he cited the "Encyclopædia Britannica" in confirmation of some statement, I had no doubt of its truth, and I resolved sometime to get my hands on that book. I still have those notes and references that I took sixty years ago.

At a much earlier stage of my mental development I had a passion for drawing, but, quite unguided, it resulted only in a waste of paper. I wanted to walk before I could creep, to paint before I could draw, and getting a box of cheap water colours, I indulged my crude artistic instincts. My most ambitious piece was a picture of General Winfield Scott standing beside his horse and some piece of artillery, which I copied from a print. It was of course an awful daub, but in connection with it I heard for the first time a new word, —the word "taste" used in its æsthetic sense. One of the neighbour women was calling at the house, and seeing my picture said to Mother, "What taste that boy has." That application of the word made an impression on me that I have never forgotten.

About this time I heard another new word. We were working on the road, and I with my hoe was working beside an old Quaker farmer, David Corbin, who used to be a school teacher. A large flat stone was turned over, and beneath it in some orderly arrangement were some smaller stones. "Here are some antiquities," said Mr. Corbin, and my vocabulary received another addition. A new word or a new thing was very apt to make its mark upon my mind. I have told elsewhere what a revelation to me was my first glimpse of one of the warblers, the black-throated blue-back, indicating as it did a world of bird life of which I had never dreamed, the bird life in the inner heart of the woods. My brothers and other boys were with me but they did not see the new bird. The first time I saw the veery, or Wilson's thrush, also stands out in my memory. It alighted in the road before us on the edge of the woods. "A brown thrasher," said Bill Chase. It was not the thrasher but it was a new bird to me and the picture of it is in my mind as if made only yesterday. Natural History was a subject unknown to me in my boyhood, and such a thing as nature study in the schools was of course unheard of. Our natural history we got unconsciously in the sport at noon time, or on our way to and from school or in our Sunday excursions to the streams and woods. We learned much about the ways of foxes and woodchucks and coons and skunks and squirrels by hunting them. The partridge, too, and the crows, hawks, and owls, and the song birds of the field and orchard, all enter into the farm boy's life. I early became familiar with the songs and habits of all the common birds, and with field mice and the frogs, toads, lizards, and snakes. Also with the wild bees and wasps. One season I made a collection of bumble-bee honey, studying the habits of five or six different kinds and rifling their nests. I kept my store of bumble-bee honey in the attic where I had a small box full of the comb and a large phial filled with the honey. How well I came to know the different dispositions of the various kinds—the small red-vested that made its nest in a hole in the ground; the small black-vested, the large black-vested, the yellow-necked, the black-banded, etc., that made their nests in old mice nests in the meadow or in the barn and other places. I used to watch and woo the little piping frogs in the spring marshes when I had driven the cows to pasture at night, till they would sit in my open hand and pipe. I used to creep on my hands and knees through the woods to see the partridge in the act of drumming. I used to watch the mud wasps building their nests in the old attic and noted their complaining cry while in the act of pressing on the mud. I noted the same complaining cry from the bees when working on the flower of the purple-flowering raspberry, what we called "Scotch caps." I tried to trap foxes and soon learned how far the fox's cunning surpassed mine. My first lesson in animal psychology I got from old Nat Higby as he came riding by on horseback one winter day, his huge feet almost meeting under the horse, just as a hound was running a fox across our upper mountain lot. "My boy," he said, "that fox may be running as fast as he can, but if you stood behind that big rock beside his course, and as he came along should jump out and shout 'hello,' he would run faster." That was the winter when in fond imagination I saw a stream of silver dollars coming my way from the red foxes I was planning to deprive of their pelts when they needed them most. I have told elsewhere of my trapping experiences and how completely I failed.

I was born at Roxbury, N. Y., April 3, 1837. At least two other American authors of note were born on the third of

April—Washington Irving and Edward Everett Hale. The latter once wrote me a birthday letter in which he said, among other things, "I have been looking back over my diaries to see what I was doing the day you were being born. I find I was undergoing an examination in logic at Harvard College." The only other American author born in 1837 is William Dean Howells, who was born in Ohio in March of that year.

I was the son of a farmer, who was the son of a farmer, who was again the son of a farmer. There are no professional or commercial men in my line for several generations, my blood has the flavour of the soil in it; it is rural to the last drop. I can find no city dwellers in the line of my descent in this country. The Burroughs tribe, as far back as I can find any account of them, were mainly countrymen and tillers of the soil. The Rev. George Burroughs, who was hung as a witch at Salem, Mass., in 1694, may have been of the family, though I can find no proof of it. I wanted to believe that he was and in 1898 I made a visit to Salem and to Gallows Hill to see the spot where he, the last victim of the witchcraft craze, ended his life. There is no doubt that the renegade preacher, Stephen Burroughs, who stole a lot of his father's sermons and set up as a preacher and forger on his own account about 1720, was a third or fourth cousin of my father's.

Farmers with a decidedly religious bent contributed the main elements of my personality. I was a countryman dyed in the wool, yea, more than that, born and bred in the bone, and my character is fundamentally reverent and religious. The religion of my fathers underwent in me a kind of metamorphosis and became something which would indeed have appeared like rank atheism to them, but which was nevertheless full of the very essence of true religion—love, reverence, wonder, unworldliness, and devotion to ideal truth—but in no way identified with Church or creed.

I used to feel that my religious temperament was as clearly traceable to the hard Calvinism of my fathers, as the stratified sandstone is traceable to the old granite rock, but that it had undergone a sea change as had the sandstone, or in my case a science change through the activity of the mind and of the age in which I lived. It was rationalism touched with mysticism and warm with poetic emotion.

My paternal grandfather and great-grandfather came from near Bridgeport in Connecticut about the end of the Revolution and settled in Stamford, Delaware County, New York. Captain Stephen Burroughs of Bridgeport, a mathematician and a man of note in his time, was Father's great uncle. Father used to say that his uncle Stephen could build a ship and sail it around the world. The family name is still common in and about Bridgeport. The first John Burroughs of whom I can find any record came to this country from the West Indies and settled in Stratford, Conn., about 1690.

He had ten children, and ten children to a family was the rule down to my own father. One October while on a cruise with a small motor boat on Long Island Sound, stress of weather compelled us to seek shelter in Black Rock harbour, which is a part of Bridgeport. In the morning we went ashore, and as we were walking up a street seeking the trolley line to take us into the city, we saw a large brick building with the legend on it—"The Burroughs Home." I felt like going in and claiming its hospitality—after our rough experience on the Sound its look and its name were especially inviting. Some descendant of Captain Stephen Burroughs was probably its founder.

My great-grandfather, Ephraim, I believe, died in 1818, and was buried in the town of Stamford in a field that is now cultivated. My grandfather, Eden Burroughs, died in Roxbury in 1842, aged 72, and my father, Chauncey A. Burroughs, in 1884 at the age of 81.

My maternal grandfather, Edmund Kelly, was Irish, though born in this country about 1765. It is from his Irish strain that I get many of my Celtic characteristics— my decidedly feminine temperament. I always felt that I was more a Kelly than a Burroughs. Grandfather Kelly was a small man, with a big head and marked Irish features. He entered the Continental army when a mere lad in some menial capacity, but before the end he carried a musket in the ranks. He was with Washington at Valley Forge and had many stories to tell of their hardships. He was upward of seventy-five years old when I first remember him—a little man in a blue coat with brass buttons. He and Granny used to come to our house once or twice a year for a week or two at a time. Their permanent home was with Uncle Martin Kelly in Red Kill, eight miles away. I remember him as a great angler. How many times in the May or June mornings, as soon as he had had his breakfast, have I seen him digging worms and getting ready to go a-fishing up Montgomery Hollow or over in Meeker's Hollow, or over in West Settlement! You could always be sure he would bring home a nice string of trout. Occasionally I was permitted to go with him. How nimbly he would walk, even when he was over eighty, and how skilfully he would take the trout! I was an angler myself before I was ten, but Grandfather would take trout from places in the stream where I would not think it worth while to cast my hook. But I never fished when I went with him, I carried the fish and watched him. The pull home, often two or three miles, tried my young legs, but Grandfather would show very little fatigue, and I know he did not have the ravenous hunger I always had when I went fishing, so much so that I used to think there was in this respect something peculiar about going fishing. One hour along the trout streams would develop more hunger in me than half a day hoeing corn or working on the road—

a peculiarly fierce, all-absorbing desire for food, so that a piece of rye bread and butter was the most delicious thing in the world. I remember that one June day my cousin and I, when we were about seven or eight years old, set out for Meeker's Hollow for trout. It was a pull of over two miles and over a pretty hard hill. Our courage held out until we reached the creek, but we were too hungry to fish; we turned homeward and fed upon the wild strawberries in the pastures and meadows we passed through and they kept us alive until we reached home. Oh, that youthful hunger beside the trout stream, was there ever anything else like it in the world!

Grandfather Kelly was a fisherman nearly up to the year of his death at the age of eighty-eight. He had few of the world's goods and he did not want them. His only vice was plug tobacco, his only recreation was angling, and his only reading the Bible. How long and attentively would he pore over the Book!—but I never heard him comment upon it or express any religious opinion or conviction. He believed in witches and hobgoblins: he had seen them and experienced them and used to tell us stories that almost made us afraid of our own shadows. My own youthful horror of darkness, and of dark rooms and recesses and cellars even in the daytime, was due no doubt largely to Grandfather's blood-curdling tales. Yet I may be wrong about this, for I remember a fearful experience I had when I was a child of three or four years. I see myself with some of the other children cowering in a corner of the old kitchen at night with my eyes fixed on the black space of the open door of the bedroom occupied by my father and mother. They were out for the evening and we were waiting for their return. The agony of that waiting I shall never forget. Whether or not the other children shared my fear I do not remember; probably they did, and maybe communicated their fear to me. I could not take my eyes off the entrance to that black cavern, though of what I may have fancied it held that would hurt me I have no idea. It was only the child's inherited fear of the dark, the unknown, the mysterious. Grandfather's stories, no doubt, strengthened that fear. It clung to me all through my boyhood and until my fifteenth or sixteenth year and was peculiarly acute about my twelfth and thirteenth years. The road through the woods at twilight, the barn, the wagon house, the cellar set my imagination on tiptoe. If I had to pass the burying ground up on the hill by the roadside in the dark, I did so very gingerly. I was too scared to run for fear the ghosts of all the dead buried there would be at my heels.

Probably I get my love for the contemplative life and for nature more through my mother than through my father; Mother had the self-consciousness of the Celt, Father not at all, though he had the Celtic temperament: red hair and freckles! The red-haired, freckled, harsh-voiced little man made a great deal of noise about the farm —shouting at the stock, sending the dog after the cows or after the pigs in the garden, or calling his orders to us in the field or shouting back his directions for the work after he had started for the Beaver Dam village. But his bark was always more to be feared than his bite. He would threaten loudly but punish mildly or not at all. But he improved the fields, he cleared the woods, he battled with the rocks and the stones, he paid his debts and he kept his faith. He was not a man of sentiment, though he was a man of feeling. He was easily moved to tears and had strong religious convictions and emotions. These emotions often found vent in his reading his hymn book aloud in a curious undulating sing-song tone. He knew nothing of what we call love of nature and he owed little or nothing to books after his schoolboy days. He usually took two weekly publications—an Albany or a New

York newspaper and a religious paper called *The Signs of the Times*, the organ of the Old School Baptist Church, of which he was a member. He never asked me about my own books and I doubt that he ever looked into one of them. How far the current of my thoughts and interests ran from the current of his thoughts and interests! Literature he had never heard of, science and philosophy were an unknown world to him. Religion (hard predestinarianism), politics (democratic), and farming took up all his thoughts and time. He had no desire to travel, he was not a hunter or fisherman, and the shows and vanities of the world disturbed him not. When I grew to crave schooling and books he was disturbed lest I become a Methodist minister—his special aversion. Religion on such easy and wholesale terms as that of his Methodist neighbours made his nostrils dilate with contempt. But literature was an enemy he had never heard of. A writer of books had no place in his category of human occupations; and as for a poet, he would probably have ranked him with the dancing master. Yet late in life, when he saw my picture in a magazine, he is said to have shed tears. Poor Father, his heart was tender, but concerning so much that fills and moves the world, his mind was dark. He was a good farmer, a helpful neighbour, a devoted parent and husband, and he did well the work in the world which fell to his lot to do. The narrowness and bigotry of his class and church and time were his, but probity of character, ready good will, and a fervent religious nature were his also. His heart was much softer than his creed. He might scoff at his neighbour's religion or politics, but he was ever ready to lend him a hand.

The earliest memory I can recall of him dates back to a spring day in my early childhood. The "hired girl" had thrown my straw hat off the stonework into the road. In my grief and helplessness to punish her as I thought she merited, I looked up to the side hill above the house and saw Father striding across the ploughed ground with a bag strung across his breast from which he was sowing grain. His measured strides, the white bag, and his regular swinging arm made a picture on the background of the red soil, all heightened no doubt by my excited state of mind, that stamped itself indelibly upon my memory. He strode across those hills with that bag suspended around his neck, sowing grain, for many years.

Another spring picture of him much later in life, when I was a man grown and home on a visit, comes to mind. I see him following a team of horses hitched to a harrow across a ploughed field, dragging in the oats. To and fro he goes all afternoon, the dust streaming behind him and the ground smoothing as his work progressed I suppose I had a feeling that I should have taken his place. He always got his crops in in season and gathered in season. His farm was his kingdom and he wanted no other. I can see him going about it, calling the dog, "hollering" at the cattle or the sheep or at the men at work in the fields, making a great deal of unnecessary noise, but always with an eye to his crops and to the best interests of the farm. He was a home body, had no desire to travel, little curiosity about other lands, except, maybe, Bible lands, and felt an honest contempt for city ways and city people. He was as unaffected as a child and would ask a man his politics or a woman her age as soon as ask them the time of day. He had little delicacy of feeling on the conventional side but great tenderness of emotion on the purely human side. His candour was at times appalling, and he often brought a look of shame into Mother's face. He had received a fairly good schooling for those times and had been a school teacher himself in the winter months. Mother was one of his pupils when he taught in Red Kill. I passed the little school house recently and wondered if there was a counterpart of Amy Kelly among the few girls I saw standing about the door, or if there was a red-haired, freckled, country greenhorn at the teacher's desk inside. Father was but once in New York, sometime in the '20's, and never saw the capitol of his country or his state. And I am sure he never sat on a jury or had a lawsuit in my time. He took an interest in politics and was always a Democrat, and during the Civil War, I fear, a "copperhead." His religion saw no evil in slavery. I remember seeing him in some political procession during the Harrison Campaign of 1840. He was with a gang of men standing up in a wagon from the midst of which rose a pole with a coon skin or a stuffed coon upon it. I suppose what I saw was part of a Harrison political procession.

Father "experienced religion" in his early manhood and became a member of the Old School Baptist Church. To become members of that church it was not enough that you wanted to lead a better life and serve

God faithfully; you must have had a certain religious experience, have gone through a crisis as Paul did, been convicted of sin in some striking manner, and have descended into the depths of humiliation and despair, and then, when all seemed lost, have heard the voice of forgiveness and acceptance and felt indeed that you were now a child of God. This crucial experience the candidate for church membership was called on to relate before the elders of the church, and if the story rang true, he or she was in due time enrolled in the company of the elect few. No doubt about its being a real experience with most of those people—a storm-and-stress period that lasted for weeks or months before the joy of peace and forgiveness came to their souls. I have heard some of those experiences and have read the record of many more in *The Signs of the Times*, which Father took for more than fifty years. The conversion was radical and lasting, these men led changed lives ever after. With them once a child of God, always a child of God, reformation never miscarried. It was an iron-clad faith and it stood the wear and tear of life well. Father was not ostentatiously religious. Far from it. I have known him to draw in hay on Sunday when a shower threatened, and once I saw him carry a gun when the pigeons were about; but he came back gameless with a guilty look when he saw me, and I think he never wavered in his Old School Baptist faith. There were no religious observances in the family and no religious instruction. Father read his hymn book and his Bible and at times his *Signs*, but never compelled us to read them. His church did not believe in Sunday-schools or in any sort of religious training. Their preachers never prepared their sermons but spoke the words that the Spirit put into their mouths. As they were mostly unlettered men the Spirit had many sins of rhetoric and logic to answer for. Their discourses did more credit to their hearts than to their heads. I recall some of their preachers, or Elders, as they were called, very distinctly—Elder Jim Mead, Elder Morrison, Elder Hewett, Elder Fuller, Elder Hubble—all farmers and unlearned in the lore of this world, but earnest men and some of them strong, picturesque characters. Elder Jim Mead usually went barefooted during the summer, and Mother once told me that he often preached barefooted in the school house. Elder Hewett was their strong man during my youth—a narrow and darkened mind tried by the wisdom of the schools, but a man of native force of character and often in his preaching attaining to a strain of true and lofty eloquence. His discourses, if their jumble of Scriptural texts may be called such, were never a call to sinners to repent and be saved— God would attend to that Himself—but a vehement justification from the Scriptures of the Old School Baptist creed, or the doctrine of election and justification by faith, not by works. The Methodists or Arminians, as he called them, were a thorn in his side and he never tired of hurling his Pauline texts at their cheap and easy terms of salvation. Could he have been convinced that he must share Heaven with the Arminians, I believe he would have preferred to take his chance in the other place. Religious intolerance is an ugly thing, but its days in this world are numbered, and the day of the Old School Baptist Society seems numbered. Their church, which was often crowded in my youth, is almost deserted now. This generation is too light and frivolous for such a heroic creed: the sons of the old members are not men enough to stand up under the moral weight of Calvinism and predestination. Absurd as the doctrine seems to us, it went with or begot something in those men and women of an earlier time—a moral fibre and depth of character—to which the later generations are strangers. Of course those men were nearer the stump than we are and had more of the pioneer virtues and hardiness than we have, and struggles and victory or defeat were more a part of their lives than they are of ours, a hard creed with heroic terms of salvation fitted their moods better than it fits ours.

My youthful faith in a jealous and vengeful God, which in some way had been instilled into my mind, was rudely shaken one summer day during a thunderstorm. The idea had somehow got into my head that if in any way we mocked the powers up above or became disrespectful toward them, vengeance would follow, quick and sure. At a loud peal overhead the boy I was playing with deliberately stuck up his scornful lips at the clouds and in other ways expressed his defiance. I fairly cringed in my tracks; I expected to see my companion smitten with a thunderbolt at my side. That I recall the incident so vividly shows what a deep impression it made upon me. But I have long ceased to think that the Ruler of the storms sees or cares whether we make faces at the clouds or not—do your work well and make all the wry faces you please.

My native mountain, out of whose loins I sprang, is called the Old Clump. It sits there with bare head but mantled sides, looking southward and holding the home farm of three hundred and fifty acres in its lap. The farm with its checkered fields lies there like a huge apron, reaching up over the smooth sloping thighs on the west and on the east and coming well up on the breast, forming the big rough mountain fields where the sheep and young cattle graze. Those mountain pastures rarely knew the plough, but the broad side-hill fields, four of them, that cover the inside of the western thigh, have been alternately ploughed and grazed since my boyhood and before. They yield good crops of rye, oats, buckwheat, and potatoes, and fair summer grazing. In winter huge snow banks lie there just below the summit of the hill, blotting out the stone fences beneath eight or ten feet of snow. I have known these banks to linger there until the middle of May. I remember carrying a jug of water one hot May day to my brother Curtis who was ploughing the upper and steepest side hill, and whose plough had nearly reached the edge of the huge snow bank. Sometimes the woodchucks feel the call of spring in their dens in the ground beneath them and dig their way out through the coarse, granulated snow, leaving muddy tracks where they go. I have "carried together" both oats and rye in all these fields. One September, during the first year of the Civil War, 1862, we were working in the oats there and Hiram was talking hourly of enlisting in the army as a drummer boy. When the cattle are grazing there, one may often see them from the road over the eastern leg of Old Clump which is lower, silhouetted against the evening sky. The bleating of the sheep in the still summer twilight on the bosom of Old Clump is also a sweet memory. So is the evening song of the vesper sparrow, which one may hear all summer long floating out from these sweet pastoral solitudes. From one of these side-hill fields, Father and his hired man, Rube Dart, were once drawing oats on a sled when the load capsized while Rube had his fork in it on the upper side trying to hold it down, and the fork with Rube clinging to it described a complete circle in the air, Rube landing on his feet below, none the worse for his adventure.

Grandfather's farm, which he and Grandmother carved out of the wilderness in the last years of 1700 and where Father was born in 1802, lies just over the hill on the western knee of Old Clump, and is in the watershed of West Settlement, a much broader and deeper valley of nearly a dozen farms, and to which my home valley is a tributary. The sugar bush lies near the groin of the old mountain, the "beech woods" over the eastern knee, and the Rundle Place, where now is Woodchuck Lodge, is on his skirts that look eastward. Hence, most of the home farm stands apart in a valley by itself. As you approach on the train from the south you may see Old Clump rising up in the north eight or ten miles away, presenting the appearance of a well-defined cone, with the upper portion of the farm showing, and hiding behind it the mountain system of which it is the southern end.

Old Clump figured a good deal in my boyhood life and scarcely less in my life since. The first deer's horn I ever saw we found there one Sunday under a jutting rock as we were on our way to the summit. My excursions to salt and count the sheep often took me there, and my boyhood thirst for the wild and adventurous took me there still oftener. Old Clump used to lift me up into the air three thousand feet and introduce me to his great brotherhood of mountains far and near, and make me acquainted with the full-chested exhilaration that awaits one on mountain tops. Graham, Double Top, Slide Mountain, Peek o' Moose, Table Mountain, Wittenburg,

Cornell, and others are visible from the summit. There was as well something so gentle and sweet and primitive about its natural clearings and open glades, about the spring that bubbled up from under a tilted rock just below the summit, about the grassy terraces, its hidden ledges, its scattered, low-branching, moss-covered maples, the cloistered character of its clumps of small beeches, its domestic looking mountain ash, its orchard-like wild black cherries, its garden-like plots of huckleberries, raspberries, and strawberries, the patches of fragrant brakes like dense miniature forests through which one wades as through patches of green midsummer snow, its divine strains of the hermit thrush floating out of the wooded depths below you—all these things drew me as a boy and still draw me as an old man.

From where the road crosses the eastern knee of Old Clump to where it crosses the western knee is over half a mile. Well down in the valley between them the home buildings are situated, and below them the old and very productive meadows, only the upper borders of which have ever known the plough. The little brooklet that drains the valley used to abound in trout, but in sixty years it has dwindled to such an extent and has been so nearly obliterated by grazing cattle that there are no trout until you reach the hemlocks on the threshold of which my fishing excursions of boyhood used to end. The woods were too dark and mysterious for my inflamed imagination —inflamed, I suppose, by Grandfather's spook stories. In this little stream in the pasture I used to build ponds, the ruins of one of which are still visible. In this pond I learned to swim, but none of my brothers would venture in with me. I was the only one in the family who ever mastered the art of swimming and I mastered it by persistent paddling in this pond on Sundays and summer evenings and between my farm duties at other times. All my people were "landlubbers" of the most pronounced type and afraid to get above their knees in the water or to trust themselves to rowboats or other craft. Here again I was an odd one.

I used to make kites and crossbows and darts and puzzle people with the trick of the buncombe blocks. One summer I made a very large kite, larger than any I had ever seen, and attaching a string fully half a mile long sent it up with a meadow mouse tethered to the middle of the frame. I suppose I wanted to give this little creature of the dark and hidden ways of the meadow —so scared of its life from hawks, foxes, and cats, that it rarely shows itself out of its secret tunnels in the meadow bottoms or its retreats under the flat stones in the pastures—a taste of sky and sunshine and a glimpse of the big world in which it lived. He came down winking and blinking but he appeared none the worse for his trip skyward, and I let him go to relate his wonderful adventure to his fellows.

Once I made a miniature sawmill by the

roadside on the overflow of water from the house spring that used to cause people passing by to stop and laugh. It had a dam, a flume, an overshot wheel ten inches in diameter, a carriage for the log (a green cucumber), a gate for the tin saw about six inches long, and a superstructure less than two feet high. The water reached the wheel through a piece of old pump log three or four feet long, capped with the body of an old tin dinner horn. Set at quite an angle, the water issued from the half-inch opening in the end of the horn with force enough to make the little wheel hum and send the saw through the cucumber at a rapid rate —only I had to shove the carriage along by hand. Brother Hiram helped me with the installation of this plant. It was my plaything for only one season.

I made a cross-gun that had a barrel (in the end of which you dropped the arrow) and a lock with a trigger, and that was really a spiteful, dangerous weapon. About my fifteenth year I had a real gun, a small, double-barrelled gun made by some ingenious blacksmith, I fancy. But it had fairly good shooting qualities—several times I brought down wild pigeons from the tree tops with it. Rabbits, gray squirrels, partridges, also fell before it. I bought it of a pedlar for three dollars, paying on the instalment plan, with money made out of maple sugar.

On the wooded west side of Old Clump we used to hunt rabbits—really the northern hare, brown in summer and white in winter. Their runways made paths among the mountain-maple bushes just below the summit. On the eastern side was a more likely place for gray squirrels, coons, and partridges. Foxes were at home on all sides and Old Clump was a favourite ground of the fox hunters. One day of early Indian summer, as we were digging potatoes on the lower side hill, our attention was attracted by someone calling from the edge of the woods at the upper side of the sheep lot. My brothers rested on their hoe handles a moment and I brushed the soil from my hands and straightened up from my bent attitude of picking up the potatoes. We all listened and looked. Presently we made out the figure of a man up by the edge of the woods and soon decided from his excited voice and gestures that he was calling for help. Finally, we made out that someone was hurt and the oxen and sled were needed to bring him down. It turned out to be a neighbour, Gould Bouton, calling, and Elihu Meeker, his uncle, who was hurt. They were fox hunting and Elihu had fired at the fox from the top of a high rock near the top of Old Clump and in his excitement had in some way slipped from the rock and fallen on the stones fifteen or twenty feet below and sustained serious injury to his side and back. With all possible speed the oxen and sled were got up there and after long waiting they returned to the house with Elihu aboard, groaning and writhing on a heap of straw. The injury had caused him to bleed from his kidneys. In the meantime Doctor Newkirk had been sent for and I remember that I feared Elihu would die before he got there. What a relief I felt when I saw the doctor coming on horseback, in the good old style, running his horse at the top of his speed! "Now," I said, "Elihu will be saved." He had already lost a good deal of blood, but the first thing the doctor did was to take more from him. This was in times when bleeding was about the first thing a doctor did on all occasions. The idea seemed to be that you could sap the strength of the disease by that means without sapping the strength of the man. Well, the old hunter survived the double blood-letting; he was cured of his injury and cured of his fox-hunting fever also.

He was a faithful, hard-working man, a carpenter by trade. He built our "new barn" in 1844 and put a new roof on the old barn. Father got out the timber for the new barn in old Jonas More's hemlocks and hauled it to the sawmill. Lanson

Davids worked with him. They had their dinner in the winter woods. One day they had a pork stew and Father said he had never eaten anything in his life that tasted so good. He and Mother were then in the flower of their days and Lanson Davids said to him on this occasion: "Chauncey, you are the biggest hog to eat I ever saw in my life." "I was hungry," said Father.

We had "raisings" in those days, when a new building was put up. The timbers were heavy, often hewn from trees in the woods, set up, pinned together in what were called "bents." In a farmer's barn there were usually four bents, tied together by the "plates" and cross beams. I remember well the early summer day when the new barn was raised. I can see Elihu guiding the corner post of the first bent and when the men were ready calling out: "All together now," "set her up," "heave'o heave, heave 'o heave," till the bent was in position.

One June when he was shingling the old barn he engaged me to pick him some wild strawberries. When I came in the afternoon with my four-quart pail nearly full he came down off the roof and gave me a silver quarter, or two shillings, as then called, and I felt very rich.

It is an open country, like an unrolled map, simple in all its lines, with little variety in its scenery, devoid of sharp contrasts and sudden changes and hence lacking in the element of the picturesque which comes from these things. It is a part of the earth's surface that has never been subject to convulsion and upheaval. The stratified rock lies horizontally just as it was laid down in the bottom of the Devonian Seas millions of years ago. The mountains and the valleys are the result of vast ages of gentle erosion, and gentleness and repose are stamped upon every feature of the landscape. The hand of time and the slow but enormous pressure of the great continental ice sheet have rubbed down and smoothed off all sharp angles, giving to the mountains their long sweeping lines, to the hills their broad round backs, and to the valleys their deep, smooth, trough-like contours. The level strata crop out here and there, giving to the hills the effect of heavy eyebrows. But occasionally it is more than that: in the mountains it is often like a cavernous mouth into which one can retreat several yards, where the imaginative farm boy loves to prowl and linger like the half savage that he is and dream of Indians and the wild, adventurous life. There were a few such cavernous ledges in the woods on my father's farm where one could retreat from a sudden shower, but less than a mile away there were two lines of them, one on Pine Hill and one on Chase's Hill, where the foundations of the earth were laid open, presenting a broken and jagged rocky front from ten to thirty or forty feet high, gnawed full of little niches and pockets and cavernous recesses by the never-dulled tooth of geologic time and affording dens and retreats where Indians and wild beasts often took refuge. As a boy how I used to haunt these places, especially on Sunday when young wintergreen and black birch gave us an excuse to go to the woods. What an eternity of time was written in the faces of those rocks! What world-old forces had left their marks there!—in the lines, in the colours, in the huge dislocations and look of impending downfall of many of them, yet with a look of calm and unconquerable age that can be felt only in the presence of such survivals of the primæval. I want no better pastime now, far from my boyhood as I am, than to spend part of a summer or autumn day amid these rocks. One passes from the sunny fields, where the cattle are grazing or the plough is turning the red furrow, into these gray, time-sculptured, monumental ruins, where the foundations of the everlasting hills are crumbling, and yet where the silence and the repose are like that of sidereal space. How relative everything is! The hills and the mountains grow old and pass away in geologic time as invariably as the snow bank in spring, and yet in our little span of life they are the types of the permanent and unchanging.

The phœbe bird loves to build its mossy nest in these shelving ledges, and once I found that one of our native mice, maybe the jumping mouse, had apparently taken a hint from her and built a nest of thistledown covered with moss on a little shelf three or four feet above the ground. Coons and woodchucks often have their dens in these ledges, and before the country was settled no doubt bears did also. In one place, under a huge ledge that projects twelve or fifteen feet, there is a spring to which cattle come from the near fields to drink. The old earth builders used material of very unequal hardness and durability when they built these hills, their contracts were not well supervised, and the result has been that the more rapid decay of the softer material has undermined the harder layers and led to their downfall. Every fifty or a hundred or two hundred feet in the Catskill formation the old contractors slipped in a layer of soft, slatey, red sandstone which introduces an element of weakness and that we everywhere see the effects of. One effect of this weakness has an element of beauty. I refer to the beautiful waterfalls that are sparsely scattered over this region, made possible, as nearly everywhere else, by the harder strata holding out after the softer ones beneath have eroded away, thus keeping the face of the falls nearly vertical.

The Catskill region is abundantly supplied with springs that yield the best water in the world. My father's farm had a spring in nearly every field, each one with a character of its own. What associations linger about each one of them! How eagerly we found our way to them in the hot haying and harvesting days!—the small, cold, never-changing spring in the barn-hill meadow under the beech tree, upon whose now decayed bowl half-obliterated initials of farm boys and hired men of thirty, fifty, and nearly seventy years ago may still be seen; the spring in the old meadow near the barn where the cattle used to drink in winter and where, with the haymakers, I used to drink so eagerly in summer; the copious spring in the bank at the foot of the old orchard which, in the severe drouths of recent years, holds out when other springs fail; the tiny but perennial spring issuing from under the huge tilted rock in the sumac field where the young cattle and the sheep of the mountain pasture drink and where we have all refreshed ourselves so many times; the spring from under a rocky eyebrow on the big side hill which is now piped to the house and which in my boyhood was brought in pine or hemlock "pump logs," and to which I have been sent so many times to clean the leaves off the tin strainer— what associations have we all of us with that spring! For over eighty years it has supplied the family with water, and not till the severe drouths of later years did it fail.

The old beech tree that stands above it is one of the landmarks of the farm. Once when a boy I saw a flock of wild pigeons disappear in its leafy interior, and then saw Abe Meeker, who worked for Father in 1840, shoot into it from the stone wall, six or seven rods below, and bring down four birds which he could not see when he fired. Three of them fell dead and one fell at his feet behind the stone wall. But I need not call the roll of all the fountains of my youth on the home farm—fountains of youth indeed! and fountain of grateful memories in my later years. I never pass any of them now but my footsteps linger by them and I clean them out if they are clogged and neglected and feel that here is a friend of other days whose face is as bright and youthful as ever.

MY FATHER
BY
JULIAN BURROUGHS

MY FATHER
BY
JULIAN BURROUGHS

THE earliest recollection that I have of Father was of one spring day when he was chasing and stoning the cat, our pet cat, who had caught a bluebird. I remember the fierce look in the cat's eyes, and her nose flattened over the back of blue, her nervously twitching tail, and the speed and strength with which Father pursued her, and the language he used, language that impressed me, at least, if not the cat, and which discredited the cat and her ancestry as well. As I remember it we rescued the bluebird, and there the picture fades. Just how Father himself looked then I do not know; doubtless, childlike, I accepted him as a matter of course, along with all the other interesting things in this world in which I was finding myself. Again I remember riding on his shoulder in the downstairs hall, as he skipped about with me, and of being face to face, on equal terms, with the hall lamp, and of telling Father that when I grew up I was going to be a king, and of Father telling me at once that they hung kings on a sour-apple tree. It was always a sour-apple tree, never a sweet one, used for hangings. So I was glad to relinquish the idea of being a king and to become instead a "finder-out of things." How Father did laugh at that! He had been telling me something of his readings in astronomy and the sciences, just at that time coming into their own, and I was so impressed and fired with emulation that I, too, declared for wanting to be "a finder-out of things," and Father would repeat it and laugh heartily. It is a joy to think of him as he was then, virile in body, full fleshed, active, leading in walking and skating and swimming—what a flood of memories! What an interest he took in all the things I did, and how often a most active part. One day in May I had gone out with our one shot of shad net, and was to try an experiment. I had told Father that I would row a ways up the river and throw out the net and then row on up to the mouth of Black Creek and fish for perch, and when the tide turned would row out and take up the net, which would catch the flood slack not far above. What he thought I do not know, for he went to Dick Martin, an experienced shad fisherman, and told him what I was going to do. Dick hastened to tell him, in alarm, that what I intended was impossible, that there was a row of old stakes out from the black barn just below the mouth of Black Creek and that my net would get fast on these and I would lose it, and perhaps come to harm besides. So Father walked the two miles, hurrying up along the steep and rocky shore, and found me just coming out from the creek. He told me what Dick had said and got into the boat and we rowed out to the net, which was acting very queerly.

"You're fast now, boy, it's just as Dick said," he exclaimed as I rowed as hard as I could for the long line of buoys. Never can I forget the hour of alarm and distress, for me, that followed. The tide turned and the loitering flood gave way to the sweeping ebb, the dark water from the creek came rushing down on us, the buoys swirled and twisted in the running water and began to disappear one by one. We quickly got hold of the end and I picked up as much as I could; then Father got hold and tried to pull the net loose. He pulled and pulled until he literally pulled the stern of the skiff under water.

"You'll have to cut the net, it is the only way," he said finally, red-faced and panting, so we did cut the net, leaving a middle section there on the old stake in the bottom of the river. There is no denying that it was thoughtful of him to come, and that he had my safety and welfare at heart. Though

I was always cautious and wise to the way of the river, something might have happened and my bones might be there beside the old stake—and what a lot I would have missed! —or as Father once so aptly expressed it: "I'm not afraid to die, but I enjoy so much living!"

He was always cautioning me, and worrying about me when I was out on the river, especially at night, and yet he took chances that I would not take. In the early days here at Riverby there was no railroad on this side of the Hudson, and to get a train one must cross the river. In summer one hung out a white flag from West Park dock and Bilyou would row over for you, but when there was ice in the river one must walk or stay home. In zero weather it was only a matter of a long walk over the ice, often facing a blast of below-zero wind, but when the March thaws had begun one took one's life very lightly to venture on the ice. The thawing water cut away the ice from underneath, leaving no mark on the surface, weakening it in spots, and if one went through, the tide swept him under the ice, where the water was at least cold enough to chill one and make death easy. On such a day Father crossed the river on a crack, for, strange to say, one of the big cracks that always come in the ice had pushed or folded down, and not up, and the water had frozen over, making a streak of triple-thick ice, and on this streak he crossed the Hudson, the ice so far gone from the sun, so honeycombed and rotten, that he could stick his cane through on either side of his crack! Another time he was crossing in early April with his dog, and when in the middle of the river, which is a full half mile wide at Riverby, busy with his thoughts, he suddenly saw his dog running for the shore, which apparently was moving away rapidly toward New York! But the shores were standing eternally still; the ice it was that moved, and was moving up with the flood tide, moving just the width of a big canal that the ice harvesters had cut above. When the tide turned, about an hour later, all the ice went out of the river.

When first Father saw some smokeless powder he was surprised at its appearance, and would not believe it was powder, until he threw some on the hot stove. I used it in our old shotgun and he was much alarmed, yet he told me that in his hunt for Thomas's Lake, of which he speaks in "Wake Robin," he loaded his little muzzle-loading gun with an entire handful of powder and then, for he felt it would burst, he held it at arm's length over his head to fire. This he did time after time, in his attempt to signal to his companions. The little gun survived the ordeal and hangs now in the gun room. With it is the little cane gun, a small shotgun that looked exactly like a cane, but which was quite effective for small birds, and which he used when making collections of birds about Washington. Strangely enough for those days, it was against the law to shoot birds, and mounted guards enforced this law. Father would tell with glee how he would shoot a bird he wanted for his collection, and in a moment the guard would come rushing up, asking who fired the shot, and Father would tell him it was just over the rise of ground, or behind those trees, or something, and off would hurry the guard while Father picked up his bird and reloaded his cane. It seems queer to us now to think of John Burroughs as shooting and mounting song birds, making collections to be set up on a tree behind glass, but he did, for in those days they were quite the proper thing, cases of them, fitting enough for museums, often being seen in private homes. I can remember taking lessons in taxidermy from Father, and of skinning and mounting wildfowl, and to-day there are a loon and a prairie chicken here in the house at Riverby that he mounted in those early years. The collections of birds he made are scattered far and wide or were destroyed long ago. All of them were shot with the little muzzle-loading cane gun or with a little muzzle-loading fowling piece: those were the days of the ramrod and wasps' or hornets' nests gathered and used for wadding, and the superstition, which Father often expressed, that if you spilled or dropped a shot in loading, it was your game shot, the one that would have killed and without which the shot would miss. I can see the fascinating-looking black powder now, scintillating as Father poured it from the palm of his short brown hand into the muzzle of the gun.

There was one quality which Father possessed to a marked degree and which I always envied him, a thing small in itself, yet which enabled him to accomplish what he did in literature, and that was the ability to lay aside the business or cares of life, as one would hang up one's hat, absolutely and completely, and turn to his writing. The world will think of him as a poet naturalist, as a gentle sage and philosopher, when he was in truth a literary craftsman, and one who could never give but a portion of his time and effort to his life's work until he was sixty years of age. I first remember him as a bank examiner. I remember his going away for trips to examine banks, of his packing his valise and putting on a white or "boiled" shirt, the gold cuff buttons, his combing his beard, the wonder and mystery of it all. Then he became a "mugwump" and the new party gave his bank-examining to someone else, and, as he expressed it, "I had to stir my stumps," and he took up the raising of fine grapes.

Just as his boyhood had the cow for its centre of interest, mine had the Delaware grape. And Father made a success of his vineyards. I can see him now summer pruning, he on one side of the row, I on the other, "pulling down" as we called the summer pruning, or he was stamping lids or tying up bundles of baskets. Many of the lids had sawdust on them which had to be blown or brushed off before they could be stamped. Father acquired the habit of blowing, and he got so used to it that he would blow anyway, whether or not the lid needed it; if it did not he would blow straight ahead and I would laugh at him for it, and he would raise his eyebrows and half smile, meaning, that it was something he could indulge himself in. He once wrote of his grandson:

I had the rare good fortune to be born in the country upon a farm and to share in the duties and responsibilities of farm life. My poor grandson John is not so lucky in this respect and he has not had to pick up potatoes and stone and gather apples and husk corn and hoe corn and spread and rake hay and drive the cows and hunt up the sheep in the mountain and spread manure and weed the garden and clean the cow stables, and so on, and go two miles through snow-choked fields and woods to school in winter and have few books to read and see no illustrated papers or magazines. John has the movies by night and his bicycle by day and a graded school to attend and a hundred aids and spurs where I had none. My fate was better than John's and I can but hope he has advantages that I did not have that may offset the advantages I had.

In this case I know that time and distance lend enchantment, for of the hard work in the vineyards Father did very little— the cultivating with a horse on days so hot that the horse was covered with lather and the dust rose in a cloud over one's perspiration-soaked clothes, the days following the spray cart with the lime and blue vitriol flying in one's face and running down one's legs, the tying in March and early April until one's fingers were raw and one's neck ached from reaching up—of all these and other tasks he knew nothing. Often he said of himself that he was lazy; and, though what he accomplished in his life stands like a monument in one sense of the word, he was lazy. Routine work, a daily grind at tasks for which he had no liking, would have shortened his days and perhaps even embittered him. Yet with what eagerness he went at his writing! For sixty years and over he found his greatest joy in his craft—as he once wrote me, "There is no joy like it, when sap runs there is no fun like writing." As he said of his books in a preface to a new edition, "Very little real 'work' has gone into them." One day out at La Jolla, California, up on the hillside overlooking the blue Pacific there was a gathering in one of the biological laboratories and the school children came trooping in. Father was asked to talk to them and among other things he asked them if a bee got honey from the flowers. "No," he said, "the bee gets nectar from the flower, a thin sweetish liquid which the bee, by processes in its own body, turns into honey." I have always suspected that Father liked to think of himself as a bee, out in the sunshine and warmth, in the fields and woods, among the flowers, gathering delightful impressions of it all which with his handicraft he could preserve in an imperishable form that others might also enjoy. And does a bee really work? Is it not doing exactly what it enjoys or wants to do? Does it have to make any conscious effort to fare forth among the flowers? Does it have to keep on doing what it dislikes to do long after it is tired out? So whether the life of John Burroughs was one long life of happiness and lazy play, or whether it was one of hard work, depends, like so many other things, on the point of view. I like to think of his long and happy life as one in which he turned all work to play, and in so doing he accomplished mightily.

Often Father tried to account for himself, how he happened to break away from the life of his family and early environment so absolutely and completely and become, not a weak, easy-going, though picturesque farmer in the farther Catskills, but a man of letters, a unique and picturesque literary craftsman. "I had it in my blood, I guess," he once said. With it he had what most of us have, the love of the woods and fields and the hunting and fishing. Trout fishing, the most delightful of all, had for him a perennial charm, and bee-hunting, too, and camping out, exploring new streams and woods. All this was fostered and developed by his farm life and early associations, and then when he became vault keeper in the Treasury Department in Washington he was shut up away from it all with nothing to do but look at the steel doors. Almost without being able to do otherwise he began to live over again the delightful days he had spent afield by writing of them. He was like an exile dreaming of his native land. Nature has a trick of casting a spell over those who spend their days with her so that when the day is gone only the memories of the delights of it remain and these become ever more beautiful and highly coloured with time. To the homesick young man, shut up in the vault in Washington, the scenes of his native hills took on a beauty and charm they never could have done had he remained there among those very hills where his eyes and senses could drink their fill every hour. It seems to me like a lucky chance that his ambition to write, already manifest and firmly fixed, took the course it did, writing about Nature.

"I must have been a sport," he says of himself—a born word worshipper, a man fired with unquenchable literary ambition a lover of the best of the world's books, born of parents who knew not the meaning even of the words. I doubt very much that any of his immediate family, that is of his own generation, read a line in any of his books. His sister told him not to write, that "it was bad for the head"— how different he was from them all is shown in an incident Mother once related, and which can be told only with a word of explanation. During the war he and Mother had gone "out home," as he always spoke of visiting the parents on the homestead, and during dinner Grandfather exclaimed: "I'd like to see Abe Lincoln hung higher than Haman and I'd like to have hold of the rope!" Father sat speechless with pain and amazement, then silently pushing back his plate he rose and silently walked from the room. Then Grandmother "went for" Grandfather. But Grandfather did not realize what he was saying, and he would have been one of the very last to have harmed Lincoln, or any one else for that matter. The incident shows how different those passionate, intense, and bitter-feeling times were from ours, and how the spread of the magazines and the illustrated papers has broadened and mellowed the feelings of the people.

Father often spoke of his joy when the *Atlantic* accepted his first article, the one on "Expression" which was attributed to Emerson—he felt a new world had opened up for him, new worlds to explore and conquer with unlimited possibilities. His ambition to write got a tremendous incentive. At that time he was teaching school at a small town near Newburgh and when Saturday came he wanted to go into the parlour for his day's work. That was the time of the supremacy of the parlour, the darkened room held sacred for special occasions, funerals, and Sunday company and such, and Mother had no notion of its order being disturbed and its sanctity profaned by such a frivolous thing as writing —she locked the door. I think Father took it as an insult, not to himself, but to his calling, a deadly insult to his god of literature, and in what to me was a fine and noble and justifiable frenzy he smashed and kicked the door into "smithereens." I applaud; I'm glad he did it; he proved himself worthy of his chosen god. Mother no doubt cried. Poor demolished door—a small and material sacrifice indeed for the great god of letters!

Those years were hard ones in many ways for Father, the years in the late '50's when he was teaching school and trying many things, trying to find himself and make a living and appease the material ambitions of Mother. One summer he spent on the old homestead and grew onions; the seed he used was poor, few came up, and a summer of hard work, for both him and Mother, came to nothing. For a time he studied medicine in the office of Doctor Hull near Ashokan, and there, sitting in the little office at a spot now just on the edge of the water of what is now the great Ashokan Reservoir, he wrote his poem, "Waiting." One cannot but marvel at the prophecy of it, the vision of the discouraged boy of twenty-five every line of which has had such a fulfilment. He tried several ventures, blindly groping, hoping for success which never came to any of them. One of his ventures was a share in a patent buckle from which he was to get rich, but from which he got losses and discouragement—in fact, he had borrowed money to go into it and on his non-payment he was arrested and brought up the river on a night boat. Waking when the boat stopped at Newburgh and finding his guard was asleep, he got up and dressed and went ashore. His arrest was not legal anyway, and soon the matter was settled.

He continued to teach, and finally, in the early years of the war, drifted to Washington. A friend of his wanted him to come, saying there were many opportunities and also holding out the inducement that he could meet Walt Whitman. Finally he got a position in the Treasury Department and from Hugh McCulloch, Secretary of the Treasury, in his "Men and Measures of Half a Century," we get a picture of the young John Burroughs seeking a job, a picture that Father said was not accurate, but which at least shows how he impressed a man used to seeing many job-seekers:

One day a young man called at my office and said to me that he understood that the force of the bureau was to be increased, and that he should be glad to be employed. I asked him if he had any recommendations. "I have not," he replied; "I must be my own." I looked at his sturdy form and intelligent face, which impressed me so favourably that I sent his name to the Secretary, and the next day he was at work as a twelve-hundred-dollar clerk. I was not mistaken. He was an excellent clerk, competent, faithful, willing.

And Father has said that of the hundred dollars a month he received, he and Mother saved just half. And the real cost of living then was as high as it is now; the actual cost of food and clothing and the manner of living have changed. Father's first book: "Notes on Walt Whitman, Poet and Person," published in 1867, now long out of print, a small brown volume with gilt lettering, was brought out in those Washington days. The book was not a success and though Father took a loss on its publication, he did not have to deduct it from his income tax. Of all that life there in Washington he has spoken so much in his books, "Winter Sunshine," "Indoor Studies," "Whitman, a Study," and so on that I will leave it and return to the vineyard here on the banks of the Hudson.

It was in 1872 that Father and Mother came here and bought about a nine-acre place, sloping from the road down to the water, living for a time, nearly a year, in a small house up by the road, during which time they were building the stone house, the building of which Father has described in "Roof-Tree." He had wanted a stone house, and here was plenty of stone, "wild stone" as a native called them, to be picked up, weathered and soft in colouring, only a short haul and a few touches with the hammer or peen needed to make them into building stone. He has often spoken of Mother's first visit to her new home, just as the foundation was nicely started, and of her grief and disappointment when she saw the size of the building. The foundation of a house, open to the sky, gives no idea of the size of the finished building, and it was in vain that Father tried to explain this. "I showed her the plans," he often said, "so many feet this way and so many that, such a size to this room and such a size to that, but it was no use, she cried and took on at a great rate." Father was bank receiver then, getting three thousand a year, and on that he was building this big, three-story stone house. He took

MY FATHER

great pleasure in it—he loved to tell of the Irish mason who went off on a drunk just when he was working on the stone chimney. Disgusted at the delay Father went up, and with hammer and trowel went at the chimney himself, and the sobering mason could see him from Hyde Park, across the river. When he was sober enough to come back and go on with his work he carefully inspected what Father had done and exclaimed, "and you are a hondy mon, ye are."

The southwest bedroom on the third floor Father was to have for his room, his study, where he could write. This room he panelled to the ceiling with native woods: maple, oak, beech, birch, tulip, and others, and I like to think of his happy anticipation, his dreams of the happy hours he would spend in this room, and of the writing he would do. But he did no writing here, for a few years later he built the bark-covered study down on the edge of the bank, then a few years later yet he built Slabsides, two miles over the low mountain. It was there, especially in the study, that he did the bulk of all his literary work.

Mother was a materialist; she never rated literary efforts very high; she often seemed to think that Father should do the work of the hired man and then do his writing nights and holidays. She could see no sense in taking the best hours of the day for "scribbling," and it was only in the later years when Father had a steady income from his writings that her point of view softened. She was what they called in those days a "good housekeeper" and she kept it so well that Father had to move out for his working hours, first to the study, then two miles away. When it came to housework, Mother possessed the quality called inevitableness to an extraordinary degree. She had a way of fastening a cloth about her head, a sort of forerunner of the boudoir cap of to-day, a means of protecting her hair from any imaginary dust, and this became a symbol, a battle flag of the goddess of housecleaning.

Father was ordered out of the library, where he did his writing, and his thread was rudely broken; it was a day when sap did not run. For a high-strung, temperamental being, hasty and quick tempered, I think he showed wonderful patience, a patience that does him great credit. And yet in many ways Mother was an invaluable helpmate, she was a balance wheel that kept their world moving steadily, and I am sure saved Father from many mistakes and extravagances.

It was only years afterward, when he began to ship grapes, that Father named his place "Riverby." He had been reading a book of adventure to me, Stevenson's "Black Arrow," and in it there was a place named "Shoreby," or "by-the-shore." This suggested the name of "Riverby," or "by-the-river," to Father for his place. So it was adopted and became the trademark, "Riverby Vineyards," an oval stamp with a bunch of grapes in the middle and the address below. It became the name of the place, the name of one of Father's books, and was stamped on the lid of every crate or basket of grapes.

Father was an absolutely honest man, honest not only in packing a crate of grapes, but honest as to his own weaknesses and shortcomings. I can never forget how he admired an exclamation attributed to General Lee at Gettysburg. Pickett had made his famous charge and his veterans had come back, a few of them, defeated, and Lee said to them, "It's all my fault, boys!" "That is the true spirit of greatness," Father said, thoughtfully. And when the *Titanic* went down in mid-ocean with such a loss of life, and the order was for the women and children first to the lifeboats, men to keep back, Father said: "That took real grit. I hope I'll never have to face such a crisis."

At another time the boys were stealing his grapes, the first Delawares, not yet ripe enough, and then scattering the bunches they could not eat along the road. Father wrapped himself in a waterproof and at dark sat down under one of the vines to wait. Strange to say, he went to sleep, and stranger still one of the boys did come, and came to the very vine under which Father was sleeping. He was instantly awake and, watching his chance, jumped up and grabbed the boy. There was a swift scrimmage, the boy breaking away and fleeing. As he went over the stone wall Father clinched him and they went over together, taking the top of the wall over on them. Father being hampered by his coat, the boy was able to break away and fled up the hill toward the road where he had left his bicycle. He was unable to get away on it, however, and ran away into the night, leaving his bicycle as hostage. In the morning when I came down I found Father like a boy with a new toy. "Come out in the wash-house and see my prisoner," he laughed, and could hardly contain himself for the fun of it all. I came, and there stood the bicycle, and Father danced a war dance about it. Later the boy came and owned up and insisted on paying something, but in all kindliness Father would not of course take any of the boy's hard-earned money. He simply explained the situation to him and I am sure the boy never came back, as he might have done if he had not been treated generously. At another time some boys from across the river were caught red-handed stealing grapes. After scaring them for a time, Father gave them some grapes and sent them home. He was always cautioning us about cutting grapes,to cut only such as we would be willing to eat ourselves not to mislead or cheat the purchaser. One of his first letters, written thirty years ago, is mainly about the vineyards—it is written on paper made to imitate birch bark, and written in a swift, up and down hand that is almost as easily read as the best printing:

Onteora Club,
July 25, 1891.

DEAR JULIAN,

I want you to write me when you receive this if the dog has turned up yet. If he has not you better drive down to Bundy's again and see if he has been there. Also tell me if the hawk flies, etc. Has there been a heavy rain, and has it done any damage to the vineyard? It rained very hard here the night I arrived. If it has damaged the vineyard I will come back. Look about and see if there is any grape rot yet. I want Zeke to send me a crate of those pears there in the currants. . . . It is very pleasant up here, but I fear I will be dined and tead and drove and walked until I am sick. I have had no good sleep yet. Mr. Johnson of the *Century* is here. We sleep in a large fine tent. It is in the woods and is just like camping out, except that we do not have a bed of boughs. It is warm and rainy here this morning. Tell me if you and your mother are going out to Roxbury, or anywhere else. Tell Northrop to send on my letters if there are any. I have not received any yet. Tell me what Dude and Zeke have been doing.

Your affectionate father,
JOHN BURROUGHS.

The dog spoken of was Dan, or Dan Bundy-ah, a pretty medium-sized dog that won Father's heart and was bought for two dollars, which seemed a big price for a dog then, of a workman who helped us in the vineyards. He was always running off home. "It breaks a dog all up to change his home, or rather household; it makes of him a citizen of the world," said Father. How he did love a nice dog! Even in his last illness he often spoke of the one we owned; he had a true feeling of comradeship for a dog.

The hawk referred to is the young marsh hawk we got from the nest and raised ourselves. I know it fell to me to supply this hawk with food: English sparrows, red squirrels, and small game, a ceaseless undertaking and one which took most of my time, so much so that Mother took me to task for it time and again. When later Father "wrote up" the hawk and got something for the article I felt that I should be paid for what I had been compelled to endure in the cause! "Fifty cents for every scolding I got," was what I demanded. "You are getting your pay now," Father replied as he watched me eat.

Did the rain do any damage to the vineyard?—Yes, that was a fear that was always present. The steep side hills would often wash very badly, the soil being carried down the hill, costing us much labour in bringing it back. When there was a slack time there was always dirt to drag up the steep slopes. I know one time some of it was carried up the hill by hand. We nailed two sticks for handles on a box and Charley and I spent days carrying this box full of dirt up a very steep spot—"just like two jackasses," Father exclaimed in fun. Though he could say in his poem—

"I rave no more 'gainst time or fate"

he did often rave against the weather, especially the "mad, intemperate," as he called them, summer showers. Once there was a hailstorm. We were "out home," and after supper Mother brought forth a telegram, saying, "I did not give you this until after you had eaten." Even I was conscious of the tactless way she did it, the household looking on. With drawn face Father slowly opened and read: "Hailstorm, grapes all destroyed." How limp Father felt! He said: "I had complimented myself when I looked at those grapes. I had seen several statements that grapes would bring a good price this fall." Well, we found that half of them could be saved and that the terrific hailstorm had extended over only two vineyards—the path of the storm not half a mile across in either direction, a curious freak, but one that in ten minutes took away all profits for the year.

If I can invent a phrase I will say that Father had the pride of humility; that is, he had the true spirit of the craftsman—pride in and for his work, and not pride of self. Nothing was too good for his art, nothing too poor for himself. The following letter, written twenty-eight years ago, gives us a glimpse of himself as he was then, alone and introspective. There evidently had been a family jar, something that came far too frequently, and Father was alone here at Riverby.

West Park,
MY DEAR JULIAN, July 24, [1893].
Your letter is rec'd. Glad you are going to try the hay field. Don't try to mow away. But in the open air I think you can stand it. It is getting very dry here. I think you had a fine shower Saturday night about eight o'clock. I stood on the top of Slide Mountain at that hour all alone and I could look straight into the heart of the storm and when it lightened I could see the rain sweeping down over the Roxbury hills. The rain was not heavy on Slide and I was safely stowed away under a rock. I left here Friday afternoon, went up to Big Indian where I stayed all night. I found Mr. Sickley and his family boarding there at Dutchers. Saturday I tried to persuade Mr. S. to go with me to Slide, but he had promised his party to go another way. So I pushed on alone with my roll of blankets on my back. I was very hot and I drank every spring dry along the route. I reached the top of Slide about two o'clock and was glad after all to have the mountain all to myself. It is very grand. I made myself a snug camp under a shelving rock. Every porcupine on the mountain called on me during the night, but I slept fairly well. I stayed till noon on Sunday, when I went down to Dutchers. I made the trip easily and without fatigue, tramping 13 miles that hot Saturday with my traps. Big Indian valley is very beautiful. Monday morning Mr. Sickley walked down to the station with me and I got home on the little boat, well paid for my trip. I doubt if I come up to

Roxbury now, I fear the air will not agree with me. Do not follow your mother's example in one respect, that is, do not think very highly of yourself and very meanly of other people; but rather reverse it— think meanly of yourself and well of other people— think anything is good enough for yourself and nothing too good for others. The berries are about done—too dry for them. I may go to Johnsons and Gilders. am not in the mood yet. Write me when you get this. Love to all.

Your affectionate father,
JOHN BURROUGHS.

In these early letters to me he always signed his name in full, something he never did later.

The blankets were two army blankets, of a blue-gray with two blackish stripes at each end: they were smoke-scented from a hundred camp fires and there were holes burned in them from sparks. They had been in many woods and forests.

The berries so lightly spoken of were those of a large patch below the study, a venture which Father made in small fruit and which he was glad enough not to repeat. The berries were too insistent in their demands; they just had to be picked over every day or they wept little reddish tears and became too soft to be shipped. When Father bought the place it was nearly all out in red berries—the old Marlboroughs and Antwerps and Cuthberts, and Father continued them until they tried his patience beyond endurance.

In winter there were no grapes or berries and for a time Father went on some lecture trips, but only for a time, for he was too nervous, too easily embarrassed, too excitable for lecturing. It took too much out of him. Somewhere, something unpleasant happened, and for a long time afterward he did not give a formal lecture, if he ever did make a formal address.

He told one of his audiences that Emerson said we gain strength by doing what we do not like to do, and everyone laughed, for it was exactly the way Father felt about his lecturing. Nevertheless, he seemed to have a pretty good time while on a lecture trip, as the following letter, written when away lecturing, will show:

Cambridge, Mass.,
Feb. 6, '96.

MY DEAR JULIAN,

Things have gone very well with me so far. I reached Boston Sunday night at 9:05. I went to the Adams house that night. Monday at 3 P. M. I went out to Lowell and spoke before the women— a fine lot of them. I got along very well. One of them took me home to dinner. I came back to the Adams house at 9 o'clock. Tuesday night I went home with Kennedy and stayed all night. Wednesday I came out to Cambridge to the house of Mrs. Ole Bull, who had sent me an invitation. I am with her now: it is raining furiously all day. To-night I am to speak before the Procopeia club, and to-morrow night before the Metaphysical Society. I met Clifton Johnson in Boston and I am going to his place on Saturday and may stay over Sunday or I may come home on the 5:04 train Sunday. . . . I saw some Harvard professors last night. I hope you and your mother keep well and live in peace and quiet. Love to you both.

Your affectionate father,
JOHN BURROUGHS.

One of the enemies we had to fight in the vineyard was the rot, the black rot, an imported disease of the grape that for a few years swept everything. Then spraying with the Bordeaux mixture of lime and copper sulphate checked and finally stopped it altogether—but it was the early sprayings that counted. One year I remember Father neglected this, in his easy, optimistic way, and later, when the rot began, spraying was in vain, and I know that I took him to task for it, to my regret now. The following letter speaks of this and of my going to college, something we did not consider until the last moment. Father, not being a college man, had not thought of it:

Lee, Mass., July 21 [1897].

DEAR JULIAN,

I rec'd your letter this morning. I am having a nice time here, but think I shall go back home this week, as the rot seems to be working in the Niagaras quite badly, and the rain and heat continue. Mr. Taylor is dead and buried. He died the day I left (Friday). Rodman likes Harvard very much and says he will do anything he can for you He says if you want to mess in Memorial Hall you ought to put your name down at once. There is a special Harvard student here, a Mr. Hickman, who is tutoring Mr. Gilder's children. I like him very much. He is in the Lawrence Scientific School— about your age and a fine fellow—from Nova Scotia.

I have been to the Johnsons at Stockbridge. Owen is in love with Yale and wants you to come there. Owen will be a writer, he has already got on the Yale "Lit." He is vastly improved and I like him much. We had a five mile walk together yesterday. Rodman I think will be a journalist. He is already one of the editors of a Harvard paper—"The Crimson" I think. The country here is much like the Delaware below Hobart. I shall stop at Salisbury to visit Miss Warner and then home Friday or Saturday. I will write to my publishers to send you Hill's Rhetoric. I think you better come home early next week and stop with me at SS. Love to all.

Your loving father,
JOHN BURROUGHS.

If the grapes fail we will try to raise the money for your Harvard expenses. At the end of 1898, I expect to get much more money from my books—at least $1,500 a year.

This last was in pencil, a postscript. Evidently Father had the grape rot in mind, but at this date, July 21st, the die was cast; there was nothing one could do then. If they had been properly sprayed in May and June one could laugh at the black rot, but very likely Father had not attended to it: that is. he had made the hired man spray. He had other fish to fry, as he often said. To me the marvel of it all is that he had so many irons in the fire and was always able to write. The different properties that Father accumulated in his lifetime were alone enough to take all his time were it not for his happy nature and wonderful faculty of being able to put them aside when the muse nudged his elbow.

First he had the place here, Riverby, to which he added another nine acres later, clearing and ditching it all and getting it all out in the best grapes, the ones that made the most work and trouble: Delawares, Niagaras, Wordens, and Moore's Early. There were other kinds tried, the once famous Gaertner, Moore's Diamond, the Green Mountain or Winchell, and so on. And currants, too, acres of them set under and between the rows of grapes, and Bartlett pears, and peaches. As I write, a picture comes to mind of Father up in a peach tree, on a high step-ladder, picking peaches, and of some girls with cameras taking his picture and all laughing and the girls exclaiming: "At the mercy of the Kodakers"—and Father enjoying the joke and picking out soft peaches for them. He liked to pick peaches. The big handsome fruit in its setting of glistening green leaves appealed to him, and as he said, "When I come to one too soft to ship I can eat it." I so vividly remember our carrying the filled baskets to the dock where they were shipped to town and Father being ahead with a basket on his shoulder and of his stumbling and going headlong, his head hanging over the steep ledge of rocks, the basket bursting in its fall and the peaches going far and wide over the rocks below. We gathered up the peaches, and Father was not hurt, though he fell so close to the top of the steep ledge that his head and shoulder hung over and his face got red in his struggle to hold himself back.

Then in the early nineties he bought the land and built Slabsides, clearing up the three acres of celery swamp; and for a while he spent much time there. "Wild Life About My Cabin" was one of the nature essays written of Slabsides. The cabin was covered with slabs, and Father wanted to give it a name that would stick, he said, one that would be easily associated with the place, and he certainly succeeded, for everyone knows of Slabsides. Uncle Hiram, Father's oldest brother, spent much time with him there, the two brothers, worlds apart in their mental make-up and their outlook, spending many lonely evenings together, Father reading the best philosophy or essays, Uncle Hiram drumming and humming under his breath, dreaming his dreams, too, but never looking at a book or even a magazine. Soon he would be asleep in his chair, and before the low-burning open fire Father would be dreaming his dreams, so many of which he made come true, listening to the few night sounds of the woods. Father tried hard to make Uncle Hiram's dreams come true. He gave him a home for many years and helped him with his bee-keeping and sympathized with him fully and understood his hope that "next year" the bees would pay and return all.

Someone caught a big copperhead, one of the meanest of all poisonous snakes, and one which is quite rare here, fortunately, and for a time Father kept it in a barrel near Slabsides. Later he grew tired of it, but he had not the heart to kill it, his prisoner. "After keeping a thing shut up and watching it every day I can't go out and kill it in cold blood," he said in half apology for his act. He told the man who worked on the swamp to carry the snake, barrel and all, up among the rocks and let him go. The man, when out of sight, promptly killed the snake. It seems to me that they were both right and the snake, though innocent himself, had to suffer.

It was about two miles to Slabsides, a good part of it through the woods, and some of it up a very steep hill. I can see Father starting off with his market basket on his arm, the basket as full of provisions and reading matter as his step was full of vigour. I'll admit he did often raid Mother's pantry, and he was not averse to taking pie and cake. In fact, he was brought up on cake largely, and always ate of it freely until these last years. "His folks," as Mother would say, always had at least three kinds of cake three times a day, and then more cake the last thing before going to bed. At Slabsides most of the cooking was done over the open fire—potatoes and onions baked in the ashes, lamb chops broiled over the coals, peas fresh from the garden—how Father did enjoy it all—the sweetness of things! He would hum:

"He lived all alone, close to the bone
Where the meat is sweetest, he constantly eatest,"

and he liked to think of this old rhyme as applying to himself.

The interior of Slabsides was finished in birch and beech poles, with the bark on them, and much of the furniture he made of natural crooks and crotches. He always had his "eye peeled," as he said, for some natural piece of wood that he could use. The bittersweet has a way of winding itself about some sapling, and as the two grow it puts a mark about the tree that makes it look as though it were twisted. One such piece, a small hemlock, is over the fireplace, and Father would tell how he told the girls who visited Slabsides that he and the hired man twisted this stick by hand. "We told them we took it when it was green," he would laugh, as he told the story, "and twisted it as you see it, then fastened it and it dried or seasoned that way—and they believed it!" and he would chuckle over it mightily.

In 1913, Father was able, with the help of a friend, to buy the old homestead at Roxbury, and then he developed one of the farmhouses there, one built long ago by his brother Curtis, and thus made the third landmark in his life, any one of which was enough to occupy the time and care of one man. He called it Woodchuck Lodge, and the last years of his life were spent largely there, going out in June and returning in October.

At the time the following letter was written, Father spent much of his time at Slabsides and his interest in both the celery and lettuce grown there, as well as the grapes at Riverby, was most keen. The black duck referred to was one I had winged and brought home; it was excessively wild until we put it with the tame ducks, whereupon, as Father expressed it, "He took his cue from them and became tamer than the tame ones."

Slabsides, July 13, '97.

MY DEAR JULIAN,

I enclose a circular from Amherst College that came to you yesterday. You would doubtless do as well or better at one of the small colleges as you would at Harvard. The instruction is quite as good. It is not the college that makes the man, but the reverse. Or you might go to Columbia this fall. You would be nearer home and have just as able instructors as at Harvard. Harvard has no first class men now. But if you have set your heart on Harvard, you would of course do just as well as a special student as if admitted to college. You would miss only non-essentials. Their sheep skin you do not want; all you want is what they can teach you.

It has rained here most of the time since you left. The grapes are beginning to rot and if this rain and heat continues we may lose all of them. If the grapes go I shall not have money for you to go away this year.

Another duck was killed Saturday night, one of the last brood. It looked like the work of a coon and I and Hiram watched all Sunday night with the gun, but nothing came and nothing came last night as we know of.

Let me know what you hear from your chum. I shall look for a letter from you to-night. It is still raining and at four o'clock the sky looks as thick and nasty as ever. It threatens to be like eight years ago when you and I were in the old house. Tell me what Mr. Tooker says, etc. I may go to Gilders the last of the week.

Your affectionate father,
JOHN BURROUGHS.

Your black duck is getting tame and does not hide at all.

It is hard for the present generation to realize what a shadow, or rather influence, the Civil War cast over the days of Father's generation. War veterans, parades, pensions, stories of the war—it coloured much of the life, civil, social, political, and even the literature of the day. Some have spoken of it, in architecture, as the General Grant Period. The "panoramas"—what has become of them? I remember visiting one with Father—you went into a building and up a flight of stairs and came out on a balcony, a round balcony in the centre, and all around was a picture of one of the battle-fields of the war, bursting shells, men charging, falling, and all, always the two flags, smoke enshrouded. It made a great impression on my boyish mind. Father knew many war veterans and together we read the impressions of his friend, Charles Benton, "As Seen from the Ranks," and he kept up the friendships he had made those years he lived in Washington.

Washington, D. C.,
Mch. 2nd. [1897.]

DEAR JULIAN,

I came on from N. Y. last night, left N. Y. at 3:30 and was here at 8:45, round trip $8, ticket good till next Monday. I had a nice time in N. Y. and improved all the time, though I was much broken of my sleep. I stayed with Hamlin Garland at the hotel New Amsterdam, I like him much, he is coming on here. I was out to dinner and to lunch every day. The *Century* paid me $125 for another short article on bird songs. I wrote it the week before my sickness. It is lovely here this morning, warm and soft like April, the roads dusty. Baker's people are all well and very kind to me. They have a large house on Meridian Hill where it was all wild land when I lived here. I shall stay here until next Monday. Write me when you get this how matters go and how your mother is. Tell Hiram you have heard from me.

Your loving father,
JOHN BURROUGHS.

When I went away to college in the fall of 1897 I was able to see our home life there at Riverby from a new angle, as one must often do, get a short distance away to get a clear perspective of a place. And it being my first time away from home Father wrote more frequently, and he dropped the formality of his earlier letters.

West Park, N. Y.,
Oct. 11. [1897.]

MY DEAR JULIAN,

Your letter was here Monday morning. I am sorry you did not send some message to your mother in it. You know how quick she is to take offence. Why not hereafter address your letters to us both —thus "Dear Father and Mother." But write to her alone next time. How about that course in Geology given by Shaler? I thought you were going to take that? I had rather you take that than any course in English Composition. Read Ruskin's "Modern Painters" when you get a chance. Read Emerson's "English Traits" and his "Representative Men."

Send me some of the pictures you took at Slabsides of the Suter girls and any others that would interest me.

I go to-day to the Harrimans at Arden for two or three days. On Saturday last I had 25 Vassar girls at SS and expect more this Saturday. Lown said Black Creek was full of ducks on Sunday—I see but few on the river. Give my love to the Suter girls. . . . Much fog here lately.

Your affectionate father,
J. B.

Ducks in Black Creek—it was tantalizing to read that! It brought back the memories of the days Father and I hunted them there—I shall never forget how impressed he was by one duck, so impressed that he spoke of it at length in an article he wrote—"The Wit of a Duck." He was paddling me up the sun-lit reaches of the Shataca on Black Creek when suddenly two dusky mallards or black ducks tore out of the willow herb and dodder and came like the wind over our heads. I was using a high-powered duck gun, and brought down both ducks, one, however, with a broken wing. The duck came tumbling down and with a fine splash struck the water, where for a moment it shone and glistened in the sun. And that was all, the duck was gone instantly, we never saw it again. What happened of course was that the duck dived, using its other wing and feet, and came up in the brush, where it hid, no doubt with only half an inch of its bill out of water. Its presence of mind, working instantly and without hesitation, caused Father to exclaim in wonder.

Father was never a sportsman in the strict sense—he never had a shotgun that was really good for anything, or any hunting dogs or hunting clothes—a pair of rubber boots used for trout fishing was as far as he got in that direction—unless the soft felt hat, gray, torn, with some flies or hooks stuck in the band, could be counted. He was an expert trout fisherman, but was not averse to using grasshoppers, worms, live bait, or caddis fly larvæ. I know we stood one day in the Shataca and Father shot and shot at the black ducks that flew overhead, and he bemoaned his lack of skill in not being able to bring them down. "Dick Martin would bring those fellows down every time," he would say. As I look back on it with the light of later experience I am sure the ducks were out of range, and the borrowed gun was a weak poor thing, not a duck gun. We built ourselves a bough house out on a little island in the swamp and got in it, crouched down, and soon some ducks came down, down, lowering their feet to drop in the water. "Don't shoot, Poppie, don't shoot!" I exclaimed, and he did not shoot, and to this day he never knew why I gave such bad advice—

I was afraid of the noise of the gun! Father thought I wanted him to wait until they were nearer. But the chance never came again and we went home duckless.

In one of his essays Father spoke of a large family as being like a big tree with many branches which, though it was exposed to the perils of the storms and all enemies of trees, had as compensation more of the sun, more places for birds and their nests, more beauty, and so on. I told him that Balzac expressed the same idea in fewer words, and for a moment he looked worried. Balzac said, "Our children are our hostages to Fate." And each way of expressing the similar idea is characteristic of the man. In many ways Father was like a wide-spreading tree—his intense nature was one that caught all the sun and beauty of life, enough and more to compensate for the sorrow and pain he knew. To adventures out-of-doors, the rise of a big trout to his fly, the sudden appearance of some large wild animal, how his whole nature would react! He was well aware of this trait and often spoke of it —in fact, he had no desire to be cold and calculating before either the unusual or beautiful in nature. Something as illustrating this trait of his comes vividly to mind: one early March day I was out duck hunting here on the Hudson and Father was watching me from shore with field glasses. He was sitting in a sunny nook beside the high rocks below the hill. I was out in the drifting ice with my duck boat, which I had painted to resemble a cake of ice, and was very carefully paddling up on a flock of about a hundred Canada geese. When I got almost within range I found my lead in the ice closed and could not get nearer, but that near by there was another lead in the ice that would take me within easy range. To get to this lead I had to back out of the one I was in, rather a ticklish performance when so near the watchful geese. I did it, however, and as I remember I got some geese. But Father on shore could not see the narrow leads in the great fields of ice;

he saw only that when near the geese I suddenly began to drift backward, and judging me by himself he said afterward: "I thought when you saw all those geese so near you got so excited you were overcome —or something—and were lying there in the bottom of that boat, helpless in the ice!"

The following three letters show how he watched the river for the migrating wild fowl:

Saturday,
Riverby, Mch. 26, [1898.]

My dear Julian,
Your letter rec'd. I enclose check for $10 as I have no bills by me. You can get it cashed at Houghton, Mifflin Co., No. 4 Park St.—ask for Mr. Wheeler. Or may be the treasurer of the college will cash it. We are all well and beginning the spring work. Hiram and I are grafting grapes, and the boys are tying up and hauling ashes. The weather is fine and a very early spring is indicated. I have not seen a wild goose and only two or three flocks of ducks. I should like to have been with you at the Sportsman's Fair. If you make those water shoes or foot boats I should advise you to follow copy—make them like those you saw.

Your sentence about the whispering of the ducks' wings, etc., was good. Ruskin invented that phrase "the pathetic fallacy." You will probably find it in your rhetoric. It was all right as applied to your sentence.

Susie is very quick witted.

The shad men are getting ready. I hope you will go and hear the lectures of the Frenchman Domnic. He is worth listening to. I shall be very glad when the Easter vacation brings you home once more, you are seldom out of my thoughts. I made two gallons of maple syrup. Walt Dumont has an auction this P. M. Nip and I are going.

Your loving father,
JOHN BURROUGHS

Nip was a fox terrier that was for years Father's constant companion, and they had many adventures together.

Riverby,
Mch. 8 [1898]

MY DEAR JULIAN,

I wish you were here to enjoy this fine spring morning. It is like April, bright, calm, warm, and dreamy, sparrows singing, robins and blue birds calling, hens cackling, crows cawing, while now and then the ear detects the long drawn plaint of the meadow lark. The ice in the placid river floats languidly by and I dare say your hunting ground is alive with ducks. I am boiling sap on the old stove set up here in the chip yard. I have ten trees tapped and lots of sap. I wish you had some of the syrup. Your mother came back yesterday and she is now busy in the kitchen, good natured as yet, if it only lasts. She has hired a girl who is expected soon. Your letter came yesterday. No doubt you will have fun acting as "supe" with the boys. It will be a novel experience. Tell me all about it. A note from Kennedy says he saw Trowbridge lately and that T is going to ask you out to see him. Go if he asks you, he is an old friend of mine and a fine man. You have read his stories when you were a boy. He has some nice girls. Remember me to him if you go.

I do not see or hear any ducks lately, I think they are slow in coming. But I must stop. Write soon.

Your loving father,
JOHN BURROUGHS.

When you get time look over my article in the March *Century*. I think the style is pretty good.

West Park Mch 2 [1898]

MY DEAR BOY,

Your letter came in due course last week and yesterday your mother was up and brought me your last letter to her. It is a great pleasure to know you keep well and in good heart and courage. I see you have pains in your arms which you vainly think the waists of girls would alleviate. But they would not, they would only increase the pains I have tried it and I know.

It is quite spring like here—blue birds and clear

bright days and half bare ground and drying roads and cackling hens. Ice still in the river down to the elbow.

Keep Lent all you can—that is slow up in your meat—not more than once a day at most. Your head will be all the clearer. I am very well since my return and am still writing. This thought came into my head as I lay in bed this morning— You go to college for two things, knowledge and culture. In the technical schools the student gets much knowledge and little culture. The sciences and mathematics give us knowledge, only literature can give us culture. In the best history we get a measure of both, we get facts and are brought in contact with great minds. Chemistry, physics, geology, etc., are not sources of culture. But Lessing, Goethe, Schiller, Shakespeare, etc., are. The discipline of mathematics is not culture in the strict sense; but the discipline that chastens the taste, feeds the imagination, kindles the sympathies, clarifies the reason, stirs the conscience and leads to self-knowledge and self-control, is culture. This we can only get from literature. Work this idea up in one of your themes and show that the highest aim of a university like Harvard should be culture and not knowledge.

Your mother is well and will soon be back. I see no ducks yet. Hiram is still on his hives and the music of his saw and hammer sounds good in my ears. I shall tap a tree to-day.

Your loving father,
J. B.

After I had been settled in Matthews Hall, Cambridge, for a time Father and Mother came to Cambridge to see me. Father said in his inimitable way that he asked Mother if she would go to this place or that, and she said "No" to each; then when he suggested Cambridge she said, "Yes." When they returned to Riverby, in the still, lonely house, they missed me, and Father wrote of it all:

Slabsides, Oct. 16, 1897.
MY DEAR JULIAN,
. . . We reached home safely Thursday night after a dusty ride and tiresome. It is very lonesome in the house. I think we both miss you now more than we did before we left home; it is now a certainty that you are fixed there in Harvard and that a wide gulf separates us. But if you will only keep well and prosper in your studies we shall endure the separation cheerfully. Children have but little idea how the hearts of their parents yearn over them. When they grow up and have children of their own, then they understand and sigh, and sigh when it is too late. If you live to be old you will never forget how your father and mother came to visit you at Harvard and tried so hard to do something for you. When I was your age and was at school at Ashland, father and mother came one afternoon in a sleigh

and spent a couple of hours with me. They brought me some mince pies and apples. The plain old farmer and his plain old wife, how awkward and curious they looked amid the throng of young people, but how precious the thought and the memory of them is to me! Later in the winter Hiram and Wilson came each in a cutter with a girl and stayed an hour or so. . . . The world looks lovely but sad, sad. Write us often.

Your affectionate father,
J. B.

"When it is too late"—how he understood, how broad were his sympathies! What anguish those words must cost all of us at some time! Father understood, I did not—and now it is too late.

West Park, N. Y.,
Nov. 7, 1897.

MY DEAR JULIAN,

If you will look westward now across New England about seven o'clock in the evening you will see a light again in my study window—a dim light there on the bank of the great river—dim even to the eye of faith. If your eye is sharp enough you will see me sitting there by my lamp, nibbling at books or papers or dozing in my chair wrapped in deep meditation. If you could penetrate my mind you would see that I am often thinking of you and wondering how your life is going there at Harvard and what the future has in store for you. I found my path from the study grass grown, nearly obliterated. It made me sad. Soon, soon, I said, all the paths I have made in this world will be overgrown and neglected. I hope you may keep some of them open. The paths I have made in literature, I hope you may keep open and make others of your own.

Your affectionate father,

J. B.

It was always a source of disappointment to Father that I did not write more, that I could not carry on his work—but this was more than he should have expected. He was an essayist, fired with a literary ambition that never faltered or grew dim for over sixty years. Once I wrote a brief introduction to a hunting story that won a prize in a sporting journal and I can never forget how pleased Father was with it— "It filled me with emotion," he said, "it brought tears to my eyes—write a whole piece like that and I'll send it to the *Atlantic*."

How he loved the telling phrase, the turn of words that was apt and made the

MY FATHER

form and substance one! I know I had a little silver cup or mug that I used at table, and when I saw my first locomotive bell slowly ringing I watched it and exclaimed, "Cup open bell." How Father did laugh and repeat it to me afterward—the childish way of expressing the strange and new in terms of the familiar and old. The small son of a friend of Father's when he first saw the ocean exclaimed, "Oh, the great rainy!" and Father would laugh over this expression and slap his sides in glee. The homely expressions always pleased him. One day some children came to see him. They had been sent by their parents with strict instructions to see "the man himself," and when they asked Father if he was "the man himself" he had a good laugh and told them he guessed he was. He always liked to tell and act out the story of the man who went down into the cellar for a pitcher of milk. In going down he fell down the stone stairs and bruised himself painfully. As he lay groaning and rubbing himself he heard his wife call, "John, did you break the pitcher?" Looking about in his anguish he saw the pitcher, unbroken. "No," he called back, gritting his teeth, "but, by thunder, I will," and seizing it by the handle he savagely smashed it over the stones. And Father understood exactly how he felt.

The deep interest he took in self-knowledge is well shown in the following letter:

Riverby, Nov. 17, 1897.
My dear Julian,

I was very sorry to hear of that "D" and "E." I was probably quite as much cut up as you were. I have been melancholy ever since I heard of it. But you will feel better by and by. . . . One thing you are greatly lacking in, as I suppose most boys are—self-knowledge. You do not seem to know what you can or cannot do, or when you have failed or succeeded. You have always been fond of trying things beyond your powers (I the same) as in the case of the boat. I think you over estimate yourself, which I never did. You thought you ought to have had an "A" in English, and were not prepared for your low mark in French and German. Do a little self-examination and nip the bud of conceit; get a fair estimate and make it too low rather than too high. I am sure I know my own weak points, see if you can't find yours. That saying of the ancients, "know thyself," is to be pondered daily. I always keep my expectations down, so that I am not disappointed if I get a "D" or an "E." My success in life has been far beyond my expectations. I know several authors who think they have not had their just deserts; but it is their own fault. I have just read this in Macaulay: "If a man brings away from Cambridge [where he graduated in eighteen hundred and twenty-two] self-knowledge, accuracy of mind and habits of strong intellectual exertion he has got the best the college can give him." That is what I think too.

Your loving father,

J. B.

Slabsides, Oct. 27. [1897.]

MY DEAR BOY,

I found your letter here yesterday on my return from N. J. whither I had gone on Saturday to visit Mr. Mabie. I was glad to hear from you. You must write at least once a week. Get the rowing pants you refer to and anything else you really need. . . . Do not try to live on less than $3.50 a week. Select the simplest and most nourishing food— meat only once a day—no pie but fruit and puddings. The weather still keeps fine here and dry; no rain yet and no heavy frosts.

Celery is most off; not more than $175 for this second crop. I am taking out the Niagaras below the hill—nothing pays but Delawares in the grape line. I have had a good deal of company as usual.

It cheers me up and keeps me from the blue devils Your mother is cleaning house and groaning as usual. I can only keep my temper by flight to SS.

Hiram goes to Roxbury to-morrow for two months or more. I shall miss him very much. He stands to me for father and mother and the old home. He is part of all those things. When he is here my chronic homesickness is alleviated.

I hope you will do some reading outside of your courses. Read and study and soak yourself in some great author for his style. Try Hawthorne or Emerson or Ruskin or Arnold. The most pregnant style of all is in Shakespeare. Go into the laboratory some day and have your strength tested. Binder says they can tell you what part is weakest. Watch your health and keep regular hours. Write us as often as you can. How I wish I was a Harvard student too.

With deepest affection,
JOHN BURROUGHS.

Doubtless it is a wise provision of Nature that we find our mates in our opposites. It is some natural law working for the good of the race, something to maintain the balance and uniformity of mankind. Certainly in many ways two people could not have been more unlike than Father and Mother. She said he was as weak as water, and he said he could get tipsy on a glass of water. He always said that Mother made the housekeeping an end in itself, and she said, "You know how he is, he never takes care of anything." How many evenings have I spent in the study when the lamp would begin to burn low for lack of oil and Father would have to run and fill it and Mother would complain, "Just like you, come mussing around after dark. Why didn't you fill it by daylight?" Ah, me, when it was daylight Father did not need the lamp! It was Mother who filled the lamps, trimmed them and polished the chimneys regularly in the afternoon, while the sun was still up; but it was Father who trimmed and filled his lamp and let it so shine that all the world might see! After all, I am not sure but what Mother was just the wife for him; he had a streak of stubborn determination along with his ambition to write that carried him through any trials of housecleaning or complaints about the housework. A wife in full sympathy with his work, who coddled him and made him think that everything he wrote was perfect, would never have done at all, nor would a selfish, extravagant, or society-mad woman. Father was temperamental, moody, irritable, easily influenced, easily led, suffering at times with attacks of melancholy, with but one fixed purpose, and that was to write. Mother was economical, thrifty, material, suspicious of people, determined to bring their ship to a snug harbour before old age, and she took the best of care of Father and held him steady and no doubt by her strength of character and firmness gave strength and firmness to his life. Their last years were most happy together and filled with a sympathy and understanding that were beautiful.

Sometimes Father would talk to himself, though but very seldom, and the following two letters are almost as though he were talking to himself. "I am far less forlorn when he is here," he says of himself and

Uncle Hiram. With all his self-analysis he
did not see that being forlorn was part of
the price he must pay for the simple but
intense joy he experienced from the beauty
of life and Nature.

W. P., Tuesday, Jan. 25 [1897].

MY DEAR JULIAN,

It still keeps mild here—snow nearly gone, but ice
in the river to the elbow. We do not get away
yet. Your mother will not stir and Hiram and
I will probably go to Slabsides, as she wants to
shut up the house.

Hiram came a week ago and stays and eats here in
the study—I am far less forlorn when he is here.
It probably seems strange to you, I know you have
never looked upon him very kindly. But you
have never seen Hiram—not the Hiram I see.
This little dull ignorant old man whom you have
seen is only a transparent mask through which I
see the Hiram of my youth, and see the old home,
the old days and father and mother and all the life
on the old farm. It is a feeling you cannot understand, but you may if you live to be old.

I hope you have given up that boat crew business
by this time. It is not the thing for you. You
do not go to Harvard for that. As I wrote you,
you have not the athletic temperament, but something finer and better. Good sharp daily exercise
you need, but not severe training. If you had been

half my age probably those cold baths would have killed you. Old men often die in the cold bath. The blood is driven in and makes too great a strain on the arteries. Write me when you get this and tell me about yourself.

Your loving father,
J. B.

Very likely what I did write told Father much more than I suspected, and he always stood ready with any advice he could give, especially about matters of health. Those were the years when he had many troubles: insomnia, neuralgia, and especially a trouble he called malaria, but which was largely autotoxemia. One doctor seared his arm with a white-hot iron in an effort to do away with the pain of the neuralgia and years afterward Father would laugh about it—"just like African medicine man, driving out the devils in my arm with a white-hot iron—the trouble was not there, it was the poison in my system from faulty elimination." When at last he did discover the source of his troubles how happy he was!

Riverby, Feb. 3 [1898]

My dear Julian,

Your letter came this morning. Winter is rugged here too. Snow about 20 inches and zero weather at night. I almost froze the top of my head up there in the old house. The ice men are scraping off the snow, ice 8 or 9 inches. Your mother is in Poughkeepsie, I was down there Monday night. I doubt if she comes to Cambridge and I am wondering whether I had better come or stay here and save my money. If you can come home on the Easter holidays perhaps I had better not come. If you get a week had you rather not come home then than to have me come now? Tell me how you feel. But I may feel different next week, I may be written out by that time. If I thought I could go on with my work there I would come at once. I am in excellent health and do not need a change. I could not do much with your English Exams. I have a poor opinion of such stuff. That is not the way to make writers or thinkers. I enclose my check for the bill which you must get receipted. Write me at once about the Easter holidays.

Your loving father,
John Burroughs.

Later when he visited me in Cambridge he wrote a daily theme, and I copied it and handed it in as my own, and it promptly came back marked "sane and sensible," the instructor quite unconsciously and unknowingly having hit upon two salient qualities of Father's style. I remember the theme he wrote was about the statue of John Harvard who sits bareheaded in the open, exposed to all weathers. Father said he always wanted to go and hold something over him to keep off the snow or sun. The life he led here and the surroundings could not produce other than wholesome and sane writing. The old house spoken of was the original farmhouse that stood up near the road—it was torn down in 1903 and a new cottage put up just below it. Father and I spent one summer there when we rented Riverby to New York people and he spent time there later as for instance:

                Saturday P. M.,
                  Jan. 29 [1898].

MY DEAR JULIAN,

Hiram and I are with the Ackers [who were living in the old house then]. I find the food and give them the rent and they do the work. I shall have peace now and it will taste good. If I come to C

when would you rather I should come? I am not
done with my writing yet but may be in eight or
ten days. Writing is like duck hunting, one doesn't
know what game he will get or when he will be back:
that is why I am undecided. I make everything
wait upon my writing. It is cold here, down to
four two mornings; good sleighing. I rec'd your
letter yesterday, I do not know about those plays
—ask Mr. Page or Rodman. I hope you are prospering
in your exams. This is the new pen, do not like
it much yet. The prospect for an ice harvest
brightens. Write.

Your loving father,
J. B

W. P.,
Saturday Jan 15 [1898]

MY DEAR JULIAN,

I was glad to get your letter and to see you in
such high feather. I hope you will keep so. Watch
your health and habits and you may. Still your
letter did not give me unmixed satisfaction. If
you knew how I dislike slang, especially the cheap
vulgar kind, you would spare me the affliction of
it. There is slang and slang. Some has wit in it
some is simply a stupid perversion of language. The
latter I dislike as I do the tobacco habit to which it
is close akin. You had so far escaped the tobacco
habit and I had hoped you would escape the slang
habit. It is not a bit more manly than the cigaret
or cigar. Some slang phrases, like "you're not in
it" or "you're off your trolley" and others, may do

in familiar conversation with friends, but "bunches of cold" or "cuts no ice" etc., are simply idiotic. When you write return me again the postal card that I may see what words I misspelled. It still keeps very mild here, but is snowing this morning. Nip and I have had some fine skating—like a mirror for over a mile here in front: but the ice is getting thin. I do not know when I will come to Cambridge. Your mother has just been passing through the winter solstice of her temper and declares she is not going anywhere. I shall get away by and by, even if she stays here. I read Balzac and enjoyed it. The first half is much the best. The ending is weak and absurd. The old miser is clearly and strongly drawn, so are most of the characters. But we do not pity or sympathize with the heroine.

How large and fine is that New Paltz girl, but probably like a big apple, she lacks flavour. . . .

Your affectionate father,

J. B.

It was very easy to see why Father disliked slang—it was a perversion of his art, and as I have said he had the true pride of the craftsman in his art. No one loved more the apt and witty expression; he was forever seeking them, and slang was something that overstepped the bounds and was therefore something truly abhorrent. Often

I have heard him tell the story with delighted relish of some men who were spending a winter night in a country hotel. Eugene Field I think it was who made the remark that so delighted Father, and J. T. Trowbridge recounts it in "My own Story." It was a bitter cold night and covers were scanty; and more than that, there were several panes out of the window. Field rummaged about in the closet and found the hoops of an old hoop skirt, just then going out of fashion, and these he hung over the broken window, saying "That will keep out the coarsest of the cold!" "Coarsest of the cold," Father would repeat the expression and laugh again. I remember his envious acknowledgment of an apt illustration: two famous wood choppers were chopping in a match to see which could fell his tree first, and so great was their skill and so swift their blows that the chips literally poured out of the tree as though it had sprung a leak. "That is good," he said of the phrase and lowered his eyes. Once we were motor-boating upon the Champlain Canal and we were delayed all day by the numbers of slow canal boats. Yet some of the lock tenders said business was very slack. One of our party commented upon this and said that there were enough canal boats as it was, that the canal seemed pretty well gummed up with them. "Pretty well gummed up with them," Father repeated over and over and laughed like a child each time. Often I complained about the stone house at Riverby, that Father in planning it did not plan to use the winter sunshine; not only were the windows not placed right but there were spruce trees in the way. "You write a book on 'Winter Sunshine' and you let none in your house," I told him and he said that if he had the winter sunshine in his house he might not have written the book. A statement which has a large element of fundamental truth, at least in his case.

In those days we had much fun skating; Father had a curious pair of old skates that he fastened on a pair of shoes so that they would not come off. These shoes he tucked, skates and all, under his arm and we were off. He would slip off his "Congress" shoes and slip on the shoes with skates attached and start over the ice, his dog running by his side. Once he rigged up an attempt at a sail with one of his army blankets and some pieces of moulding left over from building the study, but it would not work. People on shore said they thought it was some kind of a life-saving contraption in case he broke through the ice. One day in the Shataca we had as fine a skate as we ever could imagine— there had been a thaw with high water and Black Creek had flooded the swamp, the water going out over the heavily timbered Shataca back to the upland. This had then frozen and the water gone out from under it, leaving the glassy ice hanging from the boles of the trees. The ice sagged a little between the trees which gave one a most delightful up and down motion as they glided over it on skates, as near flying as one could imagine at that time.

In spirit and often in fact Father went to college with me, he attended lectures in the courses I was taking, and often when I had read a book required I sent the copy on to him to read and he would comment upon it. In the following letter he comments upon a book I had sent him, and draws at the same time a picture of days at Slabsides:

Slabsides,
Sunday, May 22 [1898].

MY DEAR SON,

The other day when I went home your mother "jumped" me about two things,—my going down to R's to lunch and my taking you to that 5 cent show in Boston. . . .

Heavy thunder showers here Thursday night, cloudy to-day. Pretty warm the last three days. The Primus is a great success. It uses rather more than one half cent's worth per hour. The Van B's with two Vassar girls were just over here. The "Iceland Fisherman" is a sweet tender pathetic story. One does not forget Yann: and what a picture of the life of those fishermen! I did not know that France had such an industry. I paddled up Black Creek again on Friday, but saw no ducks. . . . There were 35 people here last week. Write what you conclude to do about your room. The woods are nearly in full leaf now.

    Your loving father — J. B.

Comparing the life of Father's boyhood with our life here at Riverby in those days and again comparing that with the life to-day, one cannot but wonder what will be the final outcome. In a primitive society every individual knows everything about everything that he has in life; as civilization becomes more complex we become more and more specialists, more and more the thing that the economists call the "division of labour" becomes operative, and individuals go through life to-day knowing how to do but a very few of the things necessary to their existence. The early or primitive civilization produced an independent race, and individuals picturesque and unique in character. Father noticed this. He loved the old-fashioned man or woman who was so strongly individual and picturesque. I remember one such character, "Old blind Jimmy" he was called, who went about the country with a staff, and when Father saw him coming, one day "out home," he asked me to run with my camera and station myself down the road and get a picture of old blind Jimmy as he came along. I did so, and I knew at once that Jimmy knew I was there. He must have heard me in some way, and surely must have heard the purr of the focal plane shutter as I took his picture. One day in the market place in Jamaica, West Indies, there was a savage-looking man who looked the way you would imagine a pirate of the Spanish Main would look, and Father was much interested in him and asked me to get his picture—it took considerable manœuvring, but I did get him at last.

Much of the old order clung to us here at Riverby—Mother always made buckwheat cakes, we got a sack of flour from "out home" and she set the cakes to rise; I can hear the sound of the wooden spoon as she mixed them up in the evening and then set them behind the stove. Now we get the flour all ready to mix with water. No more running for buttermilk to use in them, no more having them rise over the batter pitcher during the night. Father always ate them, five or six. No day was begun in cold weather without "pancakes." And "out home" they made their own soap, but here Mother got a box of soap and carefully piled it up to dry and harden. There was a pail in the cellar for "soap grease," into which was put every scrap of fat or grease and saved until the day when the "soap man" came around and bought it. Those were the days when potatoes were less than fifty cents a bushel, eggs a dollar a hundred, and the very finest roe shad could be had for twenty-five cents. And shad nets were knit by hand. I can remember Father telling how the Manning family, who lived below the hill, knit shad nets all winter. Now one can buy the net already knit practically as cheaply as one can buy the twine. Sail boats dotted the

Hudson—sloops and schooners loitering up and down the river or tacking noisily back and forth. I know they used to get becalmed and tide-bound out here and the sailors would come ashore and raid fruit orchards. Once some of them stole a sheep and took it out to the schooner. The owner of the sheep came after the sailors with a search warrant but the mischievous sailors pulled the anchor chain up taut and tied the sheep to the chain and lowered away until the sheep, which they had butchered, was under water and the search warrant even could not find it.

"The little boat" referred to in the letter of July 24, 1893, and on which Father shipped his peaches, was a small steamer that ran from Rondout to Poughkeepsie and was more or less of a family institution when the river was open. It landed when we hailed it, at the dock at the bottom of our vineyard, and Father mostly went to town to do his shopping on "the little boat." Once he went to get his garden seeds and, coming back, a violent squall blew his basket with all his purchases overboard. I can still remember how disgusted and ruffled he appeared over it. At another time he was on this little boat when it landed at Hyde Park and a team of horses, hitched to a big wagon loaded with brick, were standing on the dock. They became frightened and began to back, in spite of the efforts of the driver to stop them. In a moment the rear wheels went over the edge of the dock and then when they felt the terrible backward pull of the wagon they sprang ahead in a desperate and vain effort to save themselves. Their hoofs beat frantically upon the plank, throwing up a shower of splinters, and though they strained every fibre of their bodies, they were drawn over to their death. Father was much upset over it. It made a vivid impression on him. "But," he said, "there was a priest who sat near me and who hardly saw it; he paid no more attention than if nothing had happened," and I feel that all priests suffered on that account in Father's estimation!

One of the ceremonies here at Riverby was the bringing in of the door mat at night. Mother did this or told me to do it—I doubt that Father would. It was brought in for fear of dampness or rain during the night, which would wet the mat and shorten its usefulness. How different from housekeeping nowadays!

Father always wore flannel shirts, of a dark gray, and these had the unfortunate habit of shrinking about the neck, so in washing them they were stretched and then dried over a milk pail—I can see them now, hanging on the line with the pail protruding from the neck. I played a cruel joke on Father one night; I was going out to the hired man's house to play cards and asked Father to leave the door open for me, which he did. It was very late when I returned, half-past nine or ten o'clock, and as I did not want to disturb any one I crept in in my most stealthy way and up to bed. In the morning Father asked me excitedly when I got in. "You must have been mighty sly about it," he said, half in admiration, half in reproach, when I told him, "for I lay awake listening for you to come in and when it got to be after ten I got up to come down and see what had become of you and I found you had come in."

It is ever true that many of the things that a man regards as important a woman does not; and conversely, many things a woman takes seriously are to a man a joke. The following gives a picture of the life here then and sums up the difference between the point of view of Father and Mother:

Thursday, May 17 [1900]
MY DEAR BOY,
I meant to have written you before this but I have been very much occupied and your mother has been wrestling with her house. She has gotten down to the ·kitchen with her cleaning. She has hired a woman who is to come next week and she wants to get the house in order for her. I have had company. On Friday afternoon "Teddy Roosevelt Jr" came and stayed until Monday morning. He

is his father in miniature. He kept me on the stretch all the time. On Saturday we went up the Shataca and cooked our dinner on the little island where you and I did. We had a good time. He climbed trees and rocks like a squirrel. He was all the time looking for something difficult to do.

May 19. I was choked off here and now I am in a pickle. We began to fix the cistern yesterday and got it half finished when the rain came—an inch and a half of water and your mother is furious —cried all night and is crying and storming yet this morning. Of course the blame is all mine. I wanted to fix it ten days ago but she said no, she wanted the water to clean house. If I and you had both died she could not have shed more tears than she has over this petty matter. I shall take to Slabsides to escape this tearful deluge. It has been very dry, no rain and no tears for six weeks. I was glad to see it come, cistern or no cistern. It has saved the hay crop and the strawberries.

The leaves are all out here and the apple blossoms fallen. Mr. and Mrs. Johnson of N. Y. came Sunday and left Monday night. Clifton Johnson came Tuesday morning and left Wednesday. Some Vassar people were coming to-day but it rains from the N. E.

Of course you can pick up no decent girl on the street and I should keep aloof from them. A decent girl would resent the advances of a stranger.

The birds are very numerous this spring.

Your loving father
I. B.

MY FATHER

In the spring of '99 Father was asked to join the E. H. Harriman Alaska Expedition, and though very reluctant he consented to go—he was historian of the expedition and his account of it appeared in the *Century* and in his book, "Far and Near." Mother had always said that "his folks" were afraid to go out of sight of the smoke of the home chimney. Something of this was in Father. He had to make himself go. He was always unhappy when leaving home and home ties. He made many new friends on this trip—John Muir, whom he liked immensely in spite of the fact that he sometimes called him a "cross-grained Scotchman"; Fuertes, the nature artist; Dallenbaugh, one of those who made the trip through the Grand Canyon with Major Powell and who wrote "A Canyon Voyage"; Charles Keeler, the poet, and many others.

Near Fort Wrangell, Alaska
June 5 [1899].

MY DEAR BOY,

Still we steam northward through these wonderful channels and mountain-locked sounds that mark this side of the continent amid such scenery as you and I never dreamed of. This morning we woke up at Fort Wrangell under a clear cold sky, like a Florida winter, some of them said, mercury 44 and snow capped peaks all around the horizon. On shore some wild flowers were blooming and weeds and shrubs had a good start. I saw swallows and heard song sparrows, not differing much from those at home. We have had fair weather most of the time since leaving Victoria but cold. I have borrowed a heavy overcoat and wish I had two. I sit at the door of my state room writing this and looking out upon the blue sparkling sea water and the snow capped and spruce mantled mountain ranges. Muir has just passed by, then Mr. Harriman racing with his children. I like him. He is a small man, about the size of Ingersoll and the same age, brown hair and moustache and round strong head. He seems very democratic and puts on no airs. 11 A. M. We are now going up the Wrangell narrows like the highlands of the Hudson, 25 miles long with snow capped peaks in the back-ground and black spruce clad hills and bends in the foreground. Ducks, geese, loons, and eagles all along. Bang, bang, go the rifles from the deck, but nothing is hurt. It is clear and still. How I wish for you! Last night at nine thirty we had such a sun-set; snow white peaks seven or eight thousand feet high riding slowly along the horizon behind dark purple walls of near mountain ranges all aflame with the setting sun. Such depths of blue and purple, such glory of flame and gold, such vistas of luminous bays and sounds I had never dreamed of.

I keep well but eat better than I sleep. Only two or three times have we felt the great throb of the Pacific through open gateways in this wall of islands. The first time it made me miss my dinner, which is not as bad as to lose it. In a week or two we shall have to face it for many days; then I shall want to go home. We have seen deer and elk from the steamer. We have reached the land of Indians and ravens. Many Indians in every town and ravens perched in rows upon the house tops. Our crowd is fearfully and wonderfully learned—all specialists. I am the most ignorant and the most untravelled man among them, and the most silent. We expect to reach Juneau to-night and I may be able to write once more—from Sitka.

I wish I knew if you were going west and how things are at home. I suppose you will be home before this can reach you. I wonder if you have had rain and if the grapes are breaking. I got me a stunning pair of shoes at Seattle—$7.50. Down in the belly of our ship are fat steers, 2 horses, a cow, a lot of sheep, hens, chickens, turkeys, etc. It looks like a farmer's barn yard down there. But I must stop, with much love to you and your mother. J. B.

We have just passed the Devil's Thumb, over 9,000 feet high. From the top rises a naked shaft 1600 feet high—this is the thumb. Our first glacier, too is here, a great mass of whitish ice settled low in the lap of the mountains.

From Sitka, June 17th, he wrote:

My dear Boy,

The steamer yesterday did not bring me a letter from you or your mother. I was much disappointed. If you had written as late as June 3rd it would have reached me. I got one from Hiram, he is well and his bees are doing well. There will be no other chance to get letters until we return the last of July. I dreamed of you last night and you told me the grapes were not doing well. I read in the papers of the heat in the east and we all wish for some of it here. I got me a heavy flannel shirt here and I feel warmer. The mercury is from 52 to 55 to-day. Dandelions are just past the height of their bloom, currant bushes just blooming, peas are up ten inches and weeds have a good start. There is no agriculture in Alaska, though potatoes do well. I have seen one cow, a yoke of oxen and a few horses. There are no roads except about one mile here. The streets of most of the towns are only broad plank sidewalks. Yet hens scratch here and roosters crow the same as at home. This town is very prettily situated; back of it rise steep, dark spruce-covered mountains, about 3,000 feet—in front of it a large irregular bay studded with tree-tufted islands, beyond that ten miles away rise snow capped peaks, from the top of which one could look down upon the Pacific. No land has been cleared except where the town stands. There may be 1,500 people here, half of them Indians. The Indians are well clad and clean and quiet and live in good frame houses. Many of them are half breeds. The forests are almost impassable on account of logs, brush, moss and rocks. We have nothing like it in the east. The logs are as high as your head and the moss knee deep. There are plenty of deer and bears here. Day before yesterday one of Mr. Harriman's daughters shot a deer. There are four nice girls in the party from sixteen to eighteen, as healthy and jolly and unaffected as the best country girls—two of Mr. Harriman's, a cousin of theirs, and a friend, a Miss Draper. Then there are three governesses and a trained nurse.

This is a land of ravens and eagles. The ravens perch on the houses and garden fences and the eagles are seen on the dead trees along shore. The barn swallow is here and the robin and red-start. One day we went down to the hot springs and I drank water just from Hades: it reeked with its sulphur fumes and steamed with its heat. I wish we had such a spring on board, it would help warm us. I have met a Hyde Park man here, De Graff. I have met four people here who read my books and two at Juneau and one at Skagway. We leave here tonight for Yakutat Bay, 30 hours at sea. I should be quite content to go home now or spend the rest of the time in the west. I would give something to know how things are with you—the vineyards and the celery and what your plans are and your mother's. I still eat and sleep well and am putting on flesh. Love to you both. Let me find letters at Portland in July. Your loving father, J. B.

Near Orca, Prince William Sound,
Alaska, June 27 [1899].

MY DEAR JULIAN,

Since I wrote you at Sitka we have come further north and spent five days in Yakutat Bay and since Saturday in this sound—have seen innumerable glaciers and lofty mountains and wild strange scenes. At Yakutat we went into Disenchantment Bay, 30 miles where no large steamer had ever gone before. This bay is a long slender arm of the sea which puts out from the head of Yakutat Bay and penetrates the St. Elias range of mountains. It was a weird grand scene. Birds were singing and flowers were blooming with snow and ice all about us. I saw a single barn swallow skimming along as at home. There were many Indians hunting seal among the icebergs.

In coming on here the ship rolled a good deal and I was not happy, though not really sick. On Saturday we entered this sound in clear sunshine and the clear skies continued Sunday and Monday. This morning it is foggy and misty. We steamed eighty miles across the sound on Sunday in the bright warm sunshine over blue sparkling waters. How we all enjoyed it! Far off rose lofty mountains as white as in midwinter, next to them a lower range streaked with snow and next to them and rising from the water a still lower range, dark with spruce forests.

Orca, where we anchored Saturday night, is a small cluster of houses on an arm of the sound where they can salmon, immense numbers of them. Two hundred men are employed there at this season

The salmon run up all the little rivers and streams, some of our party have shot them with rifles. Camping parties go out from the ship to collect birds and plants and to hunt bears and to stay two or three nights. No bears have as yet been seen. I stick to the ship. The mosquitoes are very thick on shore and besides that my face has troubled me a good deal, till the sunshine came on Sunday. I must have a taste of camp life on Kadiak Island, where we expect to be eight or ten days. Yesterday we found many new glaciers and two new inlets not down on the largest maps. We are now anchored to pick up a camping party we left on Sunday. Near us are two islands where two men are breeding blue foxes, their skins bring $20. We have seen one Eskimo here in his kyack. One can read here on deck at eleven o'clock at night. We have set our watches back six hours since leaving New York. I am rather dainty now about my eating, but keep well. I dreamed last night again about home and that the grapes were a failure. I hope dreams do go by opposites. I suppose you are shipping the currants. We get no mail. I hope to send this by a steamer from the north, said to be due. We have lectures and concerts and games and the people enjoy themselves much. I keep aloof much of the time. I hope you both keep well. Love to you both. J. B.

From Kadiak Father wrote of the "epidemic of verse writing" that broke out among the members of the expedition. It was the custom to hang the verses up in the smoking room, and on that fact, even, Father later wrote some doggerel. It was while on this expedition that he wrote, "Golden Crowned Sparrow in Alaska," one verse especially:

> But thou, sweet singer of the wild,
>   I give more heed to thee;
>   Thy wistful note of fond regret
>   Strikes deeper chords in me.

seems so strangely pathetic and like many of his moods.

Kadiak, July 5, '99.
MY DEAR JULIAN,

In trying to get off last night the ship got aground and must wait for high tide. I wrote to your mother yesterday. It is bright and lovely this morning, the mercury at 70—it is hot. I send you a jingle. Several of the men write doggerel and put it up in the smoking room, so I am doing it too. Mine is best so far. We will soon be off now, I trust you are well. I try not to worry.

> Bow westward faithful steamer
>   And show the east your heels
>   New conquests lie before you
>   In far Aleutian fields

MY FATHER

Kick high, if high you must
  But don't do so at meals,
  Oh don't do so at meals.
Your swinging it is graceful
  But I do detest your reels.

We're bound for Unalaska
  And we do not care who squeals
But mend your pace a little
  And show the east your heels
But in your waltzing with old Neptune
  Don't forget the hours of meals
  Don't forget the hours of meals
I'm sure you have no notion
  How dreadful bad it feels!

Push onward into Bering
  And hasten to the seals
One glance upon their harems
  Then take unto your heels
More steam into your boilers
  More vigor in your wheels
But in flirting with the billows
  Oh regard the hours of meals
  Do regard the hours of meals.
If in this we are exacting
  Please remember how it feels.

We're bound for Arctic waters
  And for the midnight sun
Then quicken your propeller
  And your pace into a run

We'll touch at lone Siberia
　To take a polar bear
Then hie away through Bering Straits
　And more frigid regions dare
But in all thy wild cavorting
　Oh don't forget our prayer

A noble task's before us
　And we'll do it ere we go
We'll cut the Arctic circle
　And take the thing in tow
And put it round the Philippines
And cool 'em off with snow.
Our boys will hail our coming,
　But a chill will seize the foe.
And we'll end the war in triumph
　Go you homeward fast or slow.

Kadiak, July 2, 1899.

Though this was a delightful trip, one might say, an ideal trip, he was homesick, sea sick, and, as he says of himself, of all the party the most ignorant, the most untravelled, the most silent. It was a new experience to him, this going with a crowd. I know he often spoke of the expedition's cheer, and how they would all give it when they came into stations—

> Who are we!
> Who are we!
> We're the Harriman, Harriman
> H. A. E.! H. A. E.!

and "how the people would stare at us!" Father said. He liked it, this jolly comradeship and crowd spirit, but it was new to him, almost painfully new, and though no one had more human sympathy, more tenderness and understanding with human weaknesses and shortcomings, no one had less of the crowd spirit. As he said, he kept aloof—not from aloofness but from embarrassment and shyness. Later he overcame most of this and was able to face a crowd or an audience with composure and sureness.

With this picture in mind another is recalled, one of him here at Riverby on summer days, scraping corn to make corn cakes. With an armful of green corn that he had picked, I can see him seated and with one of Mother's old aprons tucked under his beard. He would carefully cut down the rows of kernels and then with the back of a knife would scrape the milk of the corn into a big yellow bowl. He would hold the white ears in his brown hands and deftly cut each row, a look of composure and serenity in his eyes. He could eat his share of the cakes, too, and I like to think of those summer days. That fall he wrote from Slabsides:

Nov. 30, 1899

MY DEAR JULIAN,

I am over here this morning warming up and making ready for dinner. Hud and his wife and your mother are coming over soon. We are to have a roast duck and other things and I shall do the roasting and baking here. I wish you were here too. It is a cloudy day, but still and mild. I keep pretty well and am working on my Alaska trip—have already written about ten thousand words. The *Century* paid me $75 for two poems—three times as much as Milton got for "Paradise Lost." The third poem I shall weave into the prose sketch. The N. Y. *World* sent a man up to see me a couple of weeks ago to get me to write six or seven hundred words for their Sunday edition. They wanted me to write on the Thanksgiving turkey! Offered me $50—they wanted it in two days. Of course I could not do it off-hand in that way. So I fished out of my drawer an old MS, that I had rejected and sent that.

MY FATHER

They used it and sent me $30. It was in the Sunday *World* of Nov. 19.

I have sold four lots here for $225. One house will be started this fall. Wallhead and Millard of P. If I don't look out I will make some money out of this place yet. Your mother begins to look more kindly upon it. A N. Y. sculptor has bought the rock beyond the spring for $75. Van and Allie are ditching and cleaning the swamp of the Italians below here.

Photography is not an art in the sense that painting or music or sculpture is an art. It is nearer the mechanical arts. Nothing is an art that does not involve the imagination and the artistic perceptions. All the essentials of photography are mechanical —the judgment and the experience of the man are only secondary. A photograph can never be really a work of art. You can put those statements in the form of a syllogism.

I hope you are better of your cold. Some building burned up in Hyde Park early last night. Robert Gill shot himself in N. Y. the other day—suicide. We shall be very glad to see you again.

Your loving father,
J. B.

A long line of ducks just flew over going north.

The last letter from Slabsides was on May 23, 1900:

My dear Boy,

I am here surrounded by the peace and sweetness of Slabsides. I came here Saturday morning in the rain. It is a soft, hazy morning, the sun looking red through a thin layer of seamless clouds. Amasa is hoeing in the celery, which looks good, and the birds are singing and calling all about. I have got to go to N. Y. this afternoon to a dinner. I had much rather stay here, but I cannot well get out of going. . . . I begin to feel that I could get to writing again if I was left alone. I want to write a *Youth's Companion* piece called "Babes in the Woods" about some young rabbits and young blue birds Teddy* and I found.

Did you row in the races? What race are you preparing for now? It is bad business. The doctors tell me that those athletic and racing men nearly all have enlargement of the heart and die young. When they stop it, as they do after their college days, they have fatty degeneration. In anything we force nature at our peril.

When you are in Boston go into Houghton Mifflin Co. and tell them to give you my last book "The Light of Day" and charge to me. There is some good writing in it. Your loving father,

J. B.

*[The son of President Roosevelt.]

When I graduated at Harvard of course Father was there and he went to the baseball game and other things—we had a little reception in my room in Hastings. In the yard one day one of the old classes came along and among them was the new Vice-President, Theodore Roosevelt, and everyone cheered. "Yes," said Father, as we stood there that bright June day, "Teddy takes the crowd"—how little did he know the future, or guess that some day he would write a book "Camping and Tramping with Roosevelt"! Jacob Reid has said that no one who really knew Roosevelt ever called him Teddy, and I know it was so in Father's case. On his trip to the Yellowstone with the President, Father wrote:

In South Dakota, April 6, 7 P. M.
DEAR JULIAN,
We are now speeding northward over Dakota prairies. On every hand the level brown prairie stretches away to the horizon. The groups of farm buildings are from one half to a mile apart and look as lonely as ships at sea. Spots and streaks of snow here and there, fallen this morning. A few small tree plantations, but no green thing; farmers plowing and sowing wheat; straw stacks far and near; miles of corn stubble, now and then a lone school house; the roads a black line fading away in the distance, the little villages shabby and ugly. When the train stops for water a crowd of men, women, and children

make a rush for the President's car. He either speaks to them a few minutes or else gets off and shakes hands with them. He slights no one. He is a true democrat. He makes about a dozen speeches per day, many of them in the open air. As his friend and guest I am kept near him. At the banquets I sit at his table; on the platforms I sit but a few feet away, in the drives I am in the fourth carriage. If I hang back he sends for me and some nights comes to my room to see how I have stood the day. In St. Paul and Minneapolis there were fifty thousand people on the sidewalks. As we drove slowly along through the solid walls of human beings I saw a big banner borne by some school girls with my name upon it. As my carriage came up the girls pushed through the crowd and hurriedly handed me a big bouquet of flowers. The President saw it and was much pleased. . . . Other things like that have happened, so you can see your dad is honored in strange lands—more than he is at home. . . . I see prairie chickens as we speed along, and a few ducks and one flock of geese. . . . It is near sundown now and I see only a level sea of brown grass with a building here and there on the rim of the horizon. . . . We are well fed and I have to look out or I eat too much. You can see that the world is round up here. Your affectionate father,

J. B.

How well I can see Father's expression as he wrote that line. "Your dad is honoured in strange lands—more than he is at home"! and I sympathize with him fully. It has always been thus, that people of genius are least appreciated in their own home. And yet few men have the patience and gentleness that he had; few were as easy to get along with. He asked little for himself and was generous with what was his, and generous to the faults or shortcomings of others. I remember in one of those early March days the school boys raided his sap pans and Father chased and caught them, and as he overhauled one boy, the boy exclaimed pantingly, "I didn't touch your sap, Mr. Burris!" and Father laughed over it. "The little rascal was all wet down his front then with sap!" Father would then tell the story of the boy in school who was seen by his teacher eating an apple. "I saw you then," exclaimed the teacher. "Saw me do what?" said the boy. "Saw you bite that apple." "I didn't bite any apple," replied the boy. "Come here," and as the boy came up the teacher opened his mouth and took out a big chunk of apple. "I didn't know it was there," promptly said the boy. Father would always laugh at that: he sympathized with the boy. Yet when he taught school he had a big bundle of "gads" as he called them and he hid them in the stove pipe, where the boys failed to find them. I remember how Mother said that one boy imposed upon Father's good nature too far, and then when Father did finally get angry he got furious and grabbed the boy, who hung on his desk, and Father took him desk and all, tearing the desk from its floor fastenings. Doubtless afterward he was very sorry he had let his temper "get the better" of him, as he would express it.

In those days we often went for a swim, either in the river, or over to the swimming pool in Black Creek. Father was a good swimmer but he would never dive—he said it always seemed to him that there would be many water soldiers down there holding up spears, and one would be impaled upon them if he dived. Many times I have asked myself just how he looked in those days when he was so strong and active. There was something very natural about him, a thin white skin that bled easily at a scratch; fine hair that grew well and was wavy; a fine-grained, fluid kind of body, like the new growth of ferns or new shoots of willows; medium size hands, broad and brown, with fingers bent from milking when he was a small boy; picturesque in dress, everything soft and subdued in colour. Someone once said that his style in literature was slovenly, and Father said that that was true. "I am slovenly in my dress and all I do, so no doubt my style is slovenly also." Though this may seem to be a harsh criticism, it is true in the sense that Nature herself is slovenly, slovenly in contrast to what is stiff and artificial. His eyes were grayish brown, light, with a hint of green. His voice was soft and when he was embarrassed he stammered: he would force the words out.

with a little hesitation; then when the word did come it was quick and forced.

In the same way his long-enduring patience, when once it did become exhausted the temper came out in full measure. Often he was the one who suffered—more often, I should say. In the following letter he refers to the broken bone in his hand, a long and painful break, that caused him months of suffering. One day when chopping wood on his wood pile by the study a small stick irritated him, it would not lie still, but rolled about and dodged the axe until in fury Father managed to strike it. The stick flew back and in some way broke the bone in his right hand that goes to the knuckle of the index finger, which he used in writing.

At Home, Feb. 12 [1907].

DEAR JULIAN,

Your letter was forwarded me from M. I got here early Monday morning. I got my teeth Saturday. I feel as if I had a tin roof in my mouth, cornice and all. I don't know how I can ever endure them, they are horrible. . . .

I took your Hobo piece to Dr. Barrus and she read it to Miss C and me, they were both delighted with it, even enthusiastic. *Forest and Stream* has returned your piece. I enclose their letter. I have read the paper. It is not anywhere near as good as your Hobo sketch—has not the same sparkle, buoyancy, and go. You can make it better. In such an account you must put a spell upon your reader and to do this you must go more into detail and be more deeply absorbed yourself.

My hand is nearly well. Three doctors in M agreed that I had broken a bone. . . . Love to you all,

J. B.

Father always took a most lively interest in the few magazine articles I wrote and though he would never "correct" a MS. he would tell why it was good or bad, and if it was good it gave him the greatest pleasure. Once when I wrote an article called "Making Hens Lay" and showed him the cheque I received for it, he exclaimed, "*That* is the way to make hens lay!" Though he often said that if he wrote what the editors wanted him to write, very soon they would not want what he did write, he replied to my saying that Verdi's most popular opera was written to order, that a similar request from an editor gave him a hint from which he wrote one of his best essays. The controversy which Father started and which President Roosevelt joined and in which he coined the phrase "nature fakers" did Father much good in that it quickened his thoughts and stimulated him in many ways. He received many abusive letters, which only amused and entertained him, and in all it made a most interesting episode. In one of his letters from Washington he wrote: "At the Carnegie dinner I met Thompson Seton. He behaved finely and asked to sit next me at dinner. He quite won my heart." That was March 31, 1903. In checking up the statements made by the "nature fakers" Father's own power of observation was much sharpened and he became more alert. And receiving pay for articles that he wrote on the subject was an added source of fun; it was like spoils captured from the enemy. I remember well one day on the Champlain Canal we stopped at noon and Father said hilariously: "We'll all go to the hotel for dinner. We won't bother to cook dinner, we'll let the nature fakers pay for our dinner!" Like everyone else he had his blind side, things he looked at without seeing, things that had no interest or message for him. On March 1, 1908, he wrote: "That slip in the *Outlook* letter irritates me. But any one can see it was a slip of the pen—nothing can drift to windward—things drift to leeward. I see how they are laughing at me in the last number."

One first-hand observation Father made I can never forget. The joke was entirely on him, but he laughed and saw only the nature facts. In going up to Maine on a fishing expedition we had to wait for hours in the woods at a junction. While waiting we went down to a fall, where the brown waters of a small river poured down over many ledges of sandstone. In this sandstone were worn many pot-holes, some of them perfect, and of all sizes. In one about the size of a butter tub was a sucker, a measly fish about a foot long. Nothing else to do, Father pulled off his coat and rolled up his sleeves, and getting down on his knees he began to chase this sucker about the pot-hole to catch him. The sucker went around and around very deliberately until just the right moment arrived when, with a sudden burst, he threw at least half the water in the pool into Father's face. The sucker went down with the miniature flood to a larger pot-hole below. Father was soaked, choked, strangled, and blinded with the water, but when he had shaken himself and blown the water from his mouth and nose and wiped his eyes he said: "Now if that had been a trout he would have been so rattled that he would have jumped right out here on the rocks, but you see you can't rattle a sucker!"

There was one subject that Father always took seriously, and that was the question of his diet. In his youth he had known nothing of proper diet, and though the wholesome, home-made food on the farm had been the best possible thing for him, in his early manhood he had been most intemperate in his eating—"eating a whole pie at one sitting," he said. He loved to recall that when he had the measles he was ordered by the doctor to drink nothing, and when his thirst got to an unbearable point he arose, dressed, climbed out of the bedroom window and got some lemonade, of which he drank about a quart—"and I got well at once," he would add with a laugh. I wrote some verses about his eating experiments and I never knew whether he was amused or hurt. He said rather soberly, the only mention he ever made of them: "I have a new rule now, so you can add another verse to your poem."

Mother was taken sick in Georgia, where she and Father were spending the winter, the winter of 1915–16, and in March, 1917, she died here at West Park. Father had gone away. Though we all knew she could not recover, we all thought she would live until he returned, but she did not, and from Cuba, where the news reached him, he wrote a beautiful tribute. Later, after his return, we laid her to rest among her family in the little cemetery in Ton Gore, the town where Father first taught school so many years ago. One by one he had seen his family go, and many of his friends. I remember that when I told him of a princess whom Carlyle said outlived her own generation and the next and into the next, he said, "How lonely she must have been!" and much of this loneliness came into his sighs and into his thoughts as he felt himself nearing the grave. As he sat at his desk in the little study, his feet wrapped in an old coat, an open fire snapping in the fireplace, his pen turned more and more to the great question. Even in 1901 he wrote from Roxbury, at the time of the death of his sister Abigail:

I am much depressed, but must not indulge my grief, our band of brothers and sisters has not been broken since Wilson died, thirty-seven years ago. Which of us will go next? In the autumn weather in the autumn of our days we buried our sister beside her husband.

In the same letter, from his own experience he says:

I can understand your want of sympathy with the new college youth. You have learned one of the lessons of life, namely, that we cannot go back—cannot repeat our lives. There is already a gulf between you and those college days. They are of the past. You cannot put yourself in the place of the new men. The soul constantly demands new fields, new experiences.

In 1905 he wrote:

In this mysterious intelligence which rules and pervades nature and which is focussed and gathered up in the mind of man and becomes conscious of itself—what becomes of it at death? Does it fall back again into nature as the wave falls back into the ocean, to be gathered up and focussed in other minds?

During Mother's last illness she was tenderly cared for by an old friend of the family, Dr. Clara Barrus, who then took up the burden of caring for Father, not only safeguarding his health, but helping him in his literary work as well.

On November 23, 1921, we said good-bye in the station in Poughkeepsie. I looked forward to seeing him in the spring with so much joy. But he was very sad, and his hand felt frail in mine. His last letter, written in a broken, running hand, so different from the swift, virile up-and-down hand of thirty years ago, came from California, where he was urging me to join the party.

So characteristic of him and of his love of a dog and all the homely things is the line "Scratch Jack's back for me." I had written him that I was anxious to see smoke coming out of his study chimney once more, and this simple thought gave him much pleasure. But it was not to be.

La Jolla, California, Jany. 26 [1921]
DEAR JULIAN,
Your letters come promptly and are always very welcome. We all keep well. Eleanor is back

again and is driving the car. Ursie is getting fat, she drinks only filtered water, as we all do. I have had attacks of my old trouble, but a dose of Epsom salts every morning is fast curing me of them. It is still cold here and has been showery for a week or two. Shriner is painting my portrait and has got a fine thing.

We are booked to return on Mch. 25th. We shall go to Pasadena Feb. 3rd, our address there will be Sierra Madre. It is about six miles from Pasadena in Pasadena Glen. How I wish you could be here for those last two months. Yesterday Shriner took us for a long drive over in El Cajon valley and we saw a wonderful farming country, the finest I have yet seen in California, miles of orange and lemon orchards and grape vines and cattle ranches. For the past week we can see snow on the mountains nearer by than I have ever seen it. We can just see the peak of old Baldie, white as ever. As I write a big airplane is going north out over the sea.

I wish you would have Taroni or some one bring me a load of wood for my study fire.

I am bidding farewell to La Jolla and California. I never expect to return: it is too far, too expensive, and too cold. I long to see the snow again and to feel a genuine cold and escape from this "aguish" chill. I hope you all keep well. Scratch Jack's back for me. Love to Emily and Betty and John.

Your loving father,
J. B.

THE END

www.ingramcontent.com/pod-product-compliance
Lightning Source LLC
Chambersburg PA
CBHW010855090426
42737CB00019B/3374